AMERICAN WINE

AMERICAN WINE

Anthony Meisel and Sheila Rosenzweig

EXCALIBUR BOOKS

NEW YORK

A QED BOOK

First published in the USA 1983
by Excalibur Books
Distributed by Bookthrift
Excalibur is a trademark of Simon & Schuster
Bookthrift is a registered trademark of Simon & Schuster
New York, New York

ISBN 0-671-80782-X

This book was designed and produced by
QED Publishing Limited,
32 Kingly Court,
London W1.

Art director Alastair Campbell
Production director Edward Kinsey
Editorial director Jeremy Harwood
Senior editor Nicola Thompson **Art editor** Caroline Courtney
Assistant editor Sabina Goodchild **Designer** Alex Arthur
Design assistant Hilary Krag

Special photography Michael Freeman, Don Wood
Map typography Line & Line
Illustrations John Woodcock

The authors would like to thank all the many vineyard
owners and their staffs who have cooperated in this project.
Their concern and kindness have been invaluable.

Wines for the cover photograph kindly
loaned by Geoffrey Roberts Associates

Filmset in Great Britain by QV Typesetting Limited, London
Color origination by Hong Kong Graphic Arts Limited, Hong Kong
Printed in Spain by Heraclio Fournier SA, Vitoria

CONTENTS

FOREWORD

We have, in this book, tried to dispose of the jargon and high-and-mighty attitude so common to writings on wine. You will find our prejudices and opinions scattered among the mass of information. And we have tried very hard not to be too long-winded. Most of the text is devoted to the vineyards and wines themselves, over 225 vineyards across America. Some are renowned, some are barely known, but all are trying their best to produce sound, and occasionally great, wines. We have not adopted a rating system, as others have done in the past, simply because change is too rapid in the field. We feel that to do so would be unfair to the smaller vineyards and unfair to the reader. Knowledge comes from scratching under the surface, questioning, trying. Knowledge, as Norman Douglas noted, can be fun! Drinking wine should also be fun. Don't let yourself get too reverential, above all, enjoy it!

INTRODUCTION

INTRODUCTION

Wine tastes good and sometimes it is extremely good. Although this may seem obvious, too many people, especially in America, are intimidated by wine and are often unwilling to try out any drink that is unfamiliar. Some feel overwhelmed by the wide selection available today, while others are far too anxious about choosing the right wine to accompany a particular meal. Even more people are misguided by the opinion that unless a wine is expensive it is not worth drinking. However, this is not true. As we show in this book, even small vineyards that have been founded recently are now producing very drinkable wines at reasonable cost, and wine in America is fast catching up with that of France in its value and quality.

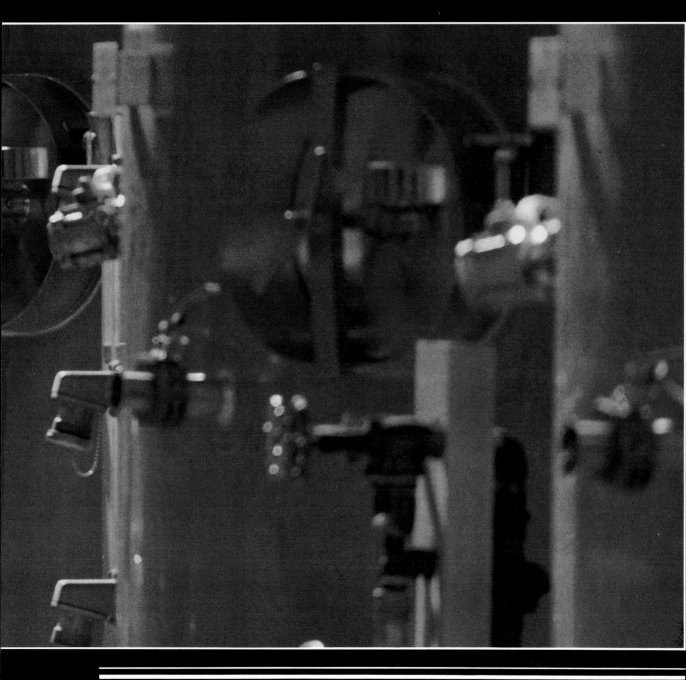

THE HISTORY OF WINE IN AMERICA

Wine is as old as recorded history, probably much older. In America, the drinking of wine arrived with the first Europeans and its cultivation began soon after. The earliest Spanish missionaries in California established vineyards about 250 years ago, yet the widespread drinking of wine is a recent phenomenon. Only since the 1960s has America started to imbibe the wines she is so capable of producing with anything like gusto.

The reason for this is not obscure. Prohibition all but put an end to the production of anything drinkable — except for sacramental wines — for 14 years. Afterward, first the economy, then the war did their utmost to discourage the making of fine wines. Furthermore, the traditional drinks of Americans have generally been beer and whiskey, with rum holding the lead in the Colonial period. In fact, in the Colonial period, drinking hard liquor was practiced with a fierce enthusiasm that would have given Carrie Nation heart failure. Everyone drank! This was largely because water supplies were not dependable. and so anything that could be fermented, was used by the Colonists to produce intoxicating beverages.

Cider was probably the first alcoholic drink to be produced in quantity as apples were there for the picking, fermentation was natural and cider was easily made. Americans enjoyed the drink and production flourished for a while.

Rum probably caused more long-term trouble than any other beverage in the history of America. In seventeenth- and eighteenth-century New England, the economy was based on "sweet things". Molasses from the West Indies was shipped to New England; there, sticky liquid rum was distilled and shipped to England. Rather than return empty-handed, the cunning Yankee captains headed down the coast of Africa to pick up slaves to take back to the West Indies to work in the sugar fields so that the molasses could be shipped north — and so the cycle continued. Economically it was a triumph of disinterested trade and would surely rank high in the pantheon of the Harvard Business School.

Rum was cheap, sweet and safe, and, unlike cider, much less was needed to bring about a state of unalloyed euphoria. Not surprisingly, cider soon went into eclipse. Cider and rum were cheap and easy to make, but rich Americans preferred to indulge their fancies, especially by drinking the luxurious vintages of the island of Madeira. John Adams and Ben Franklin could down a bottle or two of rum in an evening and George Washington was well-known for his addiction. Of course, Washington had his agent distribute close to four gallons of beer, cider, wine or rum to every voter when he ran for the Virginia legislature in 1758. And in the long tradition of political paranoia, he worried whether his hand-outs might have been on the stingy side!

Jefferson, our first Renaissance man, knew his wines, especially those of France and Germany, and he was connoisseur enough to lay down the great growths of Bordeaux and Chateau d'Yquem. But only the very rich and knowledgeable indulged in such habits. Most of the gentry drank whiskey and brandy as had their English forebears, while the common man simply drank. From awakening to bedtime, the average American, if truth be told, should have been honored for being able to stand up!

To accommodate this almost never-ending flow of "injurious" beverages, home-made berry, grain, root and flower wines were bubbling away in countless home cellars. With the introduction of the continuous still, rye and corn "likker" finally overtook and displaced rum in the hearts of

BELOW *The Great Western Winery, also known as the Pleasant Valley Wine Company, as it appeared in 1867, seven years after its founding as the first winery in New York State's famed Finger Lakes wine region.*

Americans. Everyone seemed to consider imbibing as just a license to guzzle rather than appreciate drink. Our national literature almost celebrates the kindly drunk, the vicious drunk, the forgetful drunk, the cowering drunk and the dead drunk!

During all this time the vine and its fruit were furtively holding forth. In 1769 the Franciscans established a mission at San Diego. From this time until about 1830 a small but productive wine industry flourished in California. This was a subsidized affair, however, mainly for the demands of the Church and promoting the Mission grape, a rather coarse variety. The period after the "demissionization" of California was fitful. Joseph Chapman planted vines in 1824 in Los Angeles and started selling wines in 1827, but the first real winemaker is probably Jean Louis Vignes. From Bordeaux, he planted vines on the site of the present-day L.A. railroad station and he was promoting his wines by the end of the 1830s. Others followed, but not until the advent of a Hungarian adventurer did viticulture become more than a pastime in California.

Count Agoston Haraszthy de Mokesa had, in the old country, been a man of many parts. Lawyer, farmer, soldier, bureaucrat, he also happened to be an ardent Hungarian Nationalist at a time when such creatures were not held in high regard. Fleeing the motherland, he came to America in 1839 as a political refugee. Stopping in Wisconsin along the way, he made it to the coast in 1849 and began market gardening. He then traveled to Europe shortly after 1851 and managed to collect 200,000 vine cuttings of 1,400 varieties from six countries. Returning home, he planted them in Buena Vista, California. Haraszthy had gone on this trip at the bequest of the governor (a democrat). He therefore presented his bill of $12,000 but the legislature bluntly refused to pay it. Since he was a Republican, political considerations formed an insurmountable block and he was forced to sell off the vines to cover his debts. Many vines died, many were misplanted in unsuitable locations, and many simply disappeared.

In 1862, however, he ascended to the presidency of the California Agricultural Society and marketed his first Zinfandel. Although it supposedly comes from Hungary, Zinfandel has never been traced to any other country or wine. It has become a unique California variety and produces the majority of the table wine now grown in the state. Spicy and fresh, it is the most American of wines and, when properly vinified, one of the most drinkable. Alexis Lichine has called Haraszthy "the father of California viticulture."

At the same time wine was gaining a foothold — or roothold — in two other areas, New York State and Ohio. Most famous are the sparkling wines of the Finger Lakes region of New York, which as early as 1867 were winning awards in Paris, and the winery of Nicholas Longworth in the Ohio Valley. These wines, are made from native American grape varieties. The story of the vine in America is really centered in California. The climate, the soil and sheer availability of the land, led to the early establishment of a slew of wineries: Paul Masson, Almadén, Mirassou, Charles Krug, Inglenook, Schramsberg and Beringer. By 1875 close to four million gallons a year were pouring forth from California, but within the next half-century two plagues were to devastate winemaking in America — phylloxera and Prohibition.

Between 1865 and 1890 the phylloxera, or grape louse, had managed to destroy virtually all the vines of Europe; it was no doubt imported on experimental root stocks from America. When the cuttings were reimported to the US, the plague hit with a vengeance. Much work by the California State Board of Viticultural Commissioners, commencing in 1880, helped eradicate this disease, but a number of vineyards were destroyed and abandoned forever, especially in southern California. However, the Eighteenth Amendment was far more devastating. Prohibition, from its beginning in 1919 until the jubilant day of departure in 1933, plunged America and the wine industry into a pitiful gloom.

Since the vines planted for wine ceased to be of much use after the onset of Prohibition,

The carving on this cask (ABOVE) *commemorates the*
Grand Prix won by Cresta Blanca Winery in 1889

thousands of acres were torn up to make way for table grape plantings, except for the few vineyards producing sacramental wine for the church. With Repeal, the process was reversed, though slowly. The Depression did not exactly help the production of fine wine, and with a few exceptions it was not until World War II that any great leaps were made in the production of top quality wines. Soldiers returning from Europe, having tasted wine and the good life wanted the same at home. New areas of California's North Coast were opened up to major plantings. Also, in the 1950s, new hybrid grape varieties were developed that permitted much improved wine to be made in hitherto unpromising locations.

By the 1970s, America was producing wines that could hold their own against the best Europe had to offer. Perhaps not always equal in finesse or subtlety, but that too will come in time. These top-flight wines are not cheap, nor will they ever be. The processes and care needed to produce them, and the low yield of the best varietal grapes, all combine to make them dear indeed. But to drink them with a fine meal and good company is an experience to remember.

OF WINE IN GENERAL

Wine as a beverage can be divided into the following categories: white table wines, red table wines, aperitif wines, dessert wines, sparkling wines and fortified wines. Most of this book is concerned with red and white table wines — the wines that accompany food. They, in turn, can be broken down into generic and varietal wines. A generic wine is one that is made to resemble a "type". Burgundy has a specific legal meaning in France. Any "Burgundy" produced in America is meant to resemble the original — but it is not true Burgundy. The grapes can be of any variety and they usually are. These are cheap, sound, drinkable wines of no great distinction — in other words, they are everyday wines.

In America, varietals have become the Burgundies and Bordeaux, the Graves and Sauternes of our industry. By law, the majority of grapes — 51 percent, soon to be 75 percent — must be of the variety stated on the bottle. One might think that the wine would be best if all the grapes were of that variety, but mixtures can improve the wine, as the judicious mixture of Cabernet Sauvignon and Merlot do in Bordeaux. Still, the best wines are varietal. The vintner takes the greatest care with these and some have achieved truly astounding quality.

An aperitif wine is one that is best drunk before a meal to whet the palate. Likewise, dessert wines are usually sweet, to end the meal on a more luscious note. That sweetness can come from only one thing — grape sugar. The most distinguished dessert wines are lucky in having their sugar concentrated for them by a mold, *Botrytis cinerea*, that settles on the grapes after they are ripe and draws moisture from them. When pressed, these wines have a natural sweetness — that cannot be achieved by the addition of cane or beet sugar.

Sparkling wines are the standard festive beverage, but the best are few and far between — in our opinion, no champagne-style wine produced in America approaches the best of the French Champagnes. Most sparkling wine is produced by a laborious method that in essence forces the wine into a secondary fermentation in the bottle. This is induced by freezing the top of the bottle, removing the cork, removing the sediment, adding a dosage of sugar solution and recorking the

ABOVE *These poured wines are ready for tasting. The
caps on the glasses are to prevent evaporation.*

bottle. Since this is a hand process, the wine obviously costs more. Personally, except for very dry sparkling wines as aperitifs,we feel there is always a more appropriate wine to go with any food.

Fortified wines — sherry and port, for example — are strictly for dessert. The current ad campaigns to sell cream sherries for aperitifs are pure hype — we believe that they kill the palate and to ice them is to deprive them of their character as well as put to waste all the efforts made in their production. Ficklin makes a good port, most of the American sherries being too sweet and without the smooth body necessary to elevate them beyond the merely acceptable. We feel that sherry drinking is an Anglo-Saxon pastime — fine on a frosty, damp night but certainly not before a lobster dinner.

So much for types. Whether to drink ordinary wine or fine wine is really a matter of your pocketbook. But since so much wine writing and reportage in this country is concerned with only the best, it is worth remembering the old saying: "If all women were beautiful, would there be any beautiful women?" Variety is the spice of life, and drinking different wines inevitably makes life more interesting. Vintages are occasionally mentioned in this book. There are now so many vineyards in America that it would be impossible to taste all their wines within a given year. Our advice is to seek the advice of a good wine merchant. Also, with few exceptions, very few vintages will acquire much by being laid down. Most good vineyards engage in a couple of years of bottle aging before releasing their better wines on the market, so they should be drinkable when you purchase them anyway. The great vintages of the best vineyards, especially the Cabernet Sauvignons, can be put down for anything from five to 10 years.

Whatever wine you eventually choose to buy enjoy it! Think of each bottle as a small gift — it makes it taste even better.

THE GRAPE

Without the grape, we would be in a sorry state indeed. First of all, we would be reduced to drinking grain beverages. Secondly, raisin bran would not exist. Seriously, though, without the vine and its fruit the history of mankind might have been very different. Certainly, religious ritual would be upended, the American Revolution might have taken a different tack, and you and I would be reduced to drinking diet cola with our sole Colbert.

Wines of one sort or another have been made from every known type of grape, but fine wines are made strictly from *vitis vinifera* grapes. The leading grapes in America are as follows:

Alicante Bouschet, deep red, used mostly for blending.

Barbera, from Italy, a fine soft wine improved with aging.

Cabernet Sauvignon, the grape of Bordeaux. It produces the best red varietal in California, and is best laid down for several years.

Carignane, a warm-region red grape used mainly for blending in generics.

Charbono, dark fruity wines that hold up well.

Chardonnay, the grape of great white Burgundies. It makes the finest white wine in California.

Chenin Blanc, racy, sometimes slightly sweet, but eminently drinkable white.

Emerald Riesling, fruity, tart, hybrid grape. Somewhat lacking in character. White wine.

Flora, a cross between Gewürztraminer and Semillon, not widely grown.

Folle Blanche, usually used for blending, occasionally as a varietal, crisp and acidic white.

French Colombard, usually used for blending, but increasingly as a white varietal. A bit sweet and cloying if not cooled enough.

Fumé Blanc, a white wine with sharp fruitiness.

Gamay, the grape of French Beaujolais, though the wine produced in California is often more powerful and more varietal in character.

Gamay Beaujolais, not a Gamay, but closely related to Pinot Noir. Produces a light red.

Gewürztraminer, the spicy, white wine grape of Alsace. Produces an extraordinarily flowery white of character and charm.

Green Hungarian, not Hungarian, makes for a flat ordinary wine.

Grenache, used for rosé wines, tends to be sweet without much character unless especially well-vinified.

Gray Riesling, not a Riesling. Makes an ordinary white that for some reason is quite popular in northern California.

Johannisberg Riesling, the grape of the Rhine

Vines should be planted in orderly rows (ABOVE) *with a fairly wide gap between them. This makes it easier for pickers to work unhindered at harvest time.*

and Moselle in Germany. Produces a similar wine ranging in style from light, fruity and fresh to that approaching the late-harvested, sweet wines of the mother country.

Merlot, used in Bordeaux as an integral partner to Cabernet. Increasingly for that use here where it imparts softness and complexity to otherwise harsh reds; also increasingly as a varietal for round, smooth, eminently drinkable reds.

Muscat, used for sweet dessert wines; a distinctive bouquet and underlying richness.

Petite Sirah, in reality a grape known as the Duriff. Makes soft reds of slight character.

Pinot Blanc, full-bodied dry white wines.

Pinot Noir, the great red grape of Burgundy. Not as distinguished in California as in France, the reds are lacking the complexity and depth of their overseas cousins.

Pinot St.George, minor red grape for blending or pleasant, colorful red wines.

Ruby Cabernet, pleasant, characterful reds from this cross between Cabernet and Carignane grape varieties.

Sauvignon Blanc, white wines of character and sharp fruitiness. Excellent with food.

Scheurebe, unusual, fruity white wine from a cross of Riesling grapes.

Semillon, mostly a light, crisp white wine somewhat lacking in charm.

Sirah, the true grape of the Rhône, intense, dark, warm and flavorful.

Sylvaner, used mainly for blending, but can be most agreeable when young as picnic wine.

Zinfandel, the most widely-grown grape in California, vinified into all types of reds. The experiments with the intensely varietal wines of late are not particularly successful, tending to be heavy and harsh. Best as a lighter, more flowery red, most suitable for simple food.

In harsher climes than California, other grapes are used to overcome some of the intense cold:

Aurora, a Seibel hybrid producing crisp white and sparkling wines.

Baco Noir, very strong red hybrid mostly used for blending.

Cascade, hybrid yielding a light red or rosé.

Catawba, native grape with assertive, foxy flavor which is much used for sparkling wines in New York State.

Cayuga, a cross between Seyval Blanc and Riesling makes a soft white of little character.

Chambourcin, fruity, light hybrid red.

Chancellor, middle-of-the-road drinkable reds.

Chelois, fruity reds with some residual foxiness.

Concord, leave it to the kids! Mostly for sweetened kosher-type red wines.

Cynthiana, red, South-Central grape, a native but without the usual foxiness.

De Chaunac, pleasant red hybrid, with reasonable body and color.

Delaware, a native white of clean quality. Usually pleasant.

Dutchess, New York grape similar to Delaware.

Foch, hybrid for full, soft reds. Sometimes called Maréchal Foch.

Isabella, a native used for New York State sparkling wines, little to recommend it otherwise.

Niagara, native, sweet whites.

Seyval Blanc, hybrid for full-bodied, crisp, dry white wines.

Verdelet, a fairly new hybrid for light, rather flowery white wines.

Once the grape has been chosen, the vintner must go about actually planting, growing, pruning, waiting and harvesting. And, unlike raising a pot of chives on the windowsill, the growing of vines is a process as complicated as the making of wine. Increasingly, in fact, some of the better vintners who buy grapes, such as Joe Heitz, will specifically name the vineyard from which the grapes came.

In growing wine, the climate is perhaps the first consideration. Though over 5,000 grape varieties grow in the world, the best, those that make the finest wines, will grow only under the most delicately balanced conditions. The vines can stand cold in the winter when they are dormant, but come spring, the slightest frost once budding has commenced can spell death to the crop. Until May of the growing year, ample rain is needed to penetrate deep into the soil. But after that, too much rain will make for rot, mildew and disaster again. In fact, a good winemaker is by necessity almost a professional meteorologist.

Since climate is so important, there are relatively few areas in the world where great wines can grow. And within those few regions — California and increasingly in other states, France, Germany, Italy, Spain — the soil will also dictate the grape variety and the quality of what it produces, just as the grain a chicken is fed affects its flavor. By and large, vines need well-drained, pebbly soil, preferably mountain-slope soil to soak in the rich nutrients and minerals necessary for their well-being. The combination of soil, climate and rainfall producing the best wines is rarely achieved, and it is extremely expensive to cultivate the wine in these perfect locations. Thus the high cost of the best wines.

The vine itself is a creeper. It must be trained away from the ground to avoid insects and rot, and to produce deeper roots and heavier leaves to absorb sun and protect the grapes. Since doing this involves care and time, a vine takes from five to seven years to reach a point where it can successfully produce good wine grapes. When cared for, a vine will continue to produce for 25 to 45 years at its peak. The key to this is careful pruning and cultivation — too much pruning and the vine will be useless, too little and the grapes will explode in a profusion of watery, thin wine. Pruning is an art, and each grape type and set of conditions dictates the methods and severity of the pruning.

Similarly, the cultivation of the vineyards is vital to protect the vines from pests, frost and disease. Keeping the soil clean, moist and aerated will help the vines get the nourishment they need. Fertilizing also demands precision in application since in most locations the soil varies from place to place. Too much fertilizer will cause a vine to overproduce and acquire the taste of the trace elements in the fertilizer. Too little will damage the vine.

Finally, providing all the above has been done with knowledge and care, the grapes will grow, mature, and be ready for harvesting. Here the judgement of the winemaker is paramount. Picked too soon, the grapes will not contain enough sugar to allow full fermentation. Picked too late, they will have taken up too much moisture and will be unbalanced. The skill of the winemaker can make or break the quality of the finished product.

INTRODUCTION

BELOW *Of the thousands of strains of* vinis vinifera, *only a few are capable of producing great wines. Shown here are some of the many varieties that are used in American winemaking.*

Pinot Noir

Cabernet Sauvignon

Zinfandel

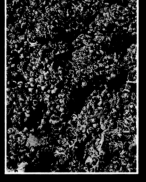

Gamay

Merlot

Chardonnay

Scheurebe

Johannisberg Riesling

Gewürztraminer

HOW WINE IS MADE

No matter what the grape, from what soil or climate, wine is made in much the same way around the world. What makes one wine different from another, or better than another, is much more a function of human judgment on the part of the winemaker than radical changes in the mechanical and chemical process.

Once the grapes arrive at the winery they are usually emptied into a hopper from whence they are fed into a stemming-crushing machine. Rotating paddles separate the stems from the grapes, and the stems are ejected as the grapes fall through a perforated drum. From this point juice can be made. The grapes are passed through rollers — gently — to break the skins and allow the juices to begin flowing. The must, a combination of juice, skins and seeds, is sent to fermenting tanks (though for white wine the process is somewhat different, as will be explained later).

Once the must arrives in the fermenting tank — stainless steel or wood, concrete-lined or not — it can either be left alone to begin fermentation on its own or it can be inoculated with special strains of yeast. In either case, the naturally occurring or special yeasts work to convert the must into more or less equal parts of carbon dioxide and alcohol. Since the sugar content determines the alcohol content, grapes which contain, say, 25 percent sugar will produce a wine of about 13.5 percent alcohol.

During the fermentation process a great deal of heat is produced. So that the wine is not ruined from excessive heat — cooked, as it were — the tanks are equipped with cooling apparatus. When the winemaker judges the time right for the completion of fermentation, he draws off the wine, leaving the sediment in the bottom of the tank. In making red wine, the sediment is sent to the presses. With whites, it is discarded.

Red wines are fermented at somewhat higher temperatures than whites, usually at about 70 to 80 degrees Fahrenheit. Fermentation at this stage takes about a week. During this time, the skins, buoyed up by the released carbon dioxide, rise to the surface of the wine and make a "hat" or cap. The wine is drawn off and pumped over this cover regularly to receive the most color and

BELOW *Among the factors in winemaking are the microclimate, the soil and the skill of the winemaker.*

White wine and brandy are made by crushing and stemming grapes (1), then pressing (2) to obtain juice for fermenting (3), which will eventually produce sweet wine (7) and sparkling wine for controlled fermenting in bottles (8). The sugar in the juice is fermented further to produce dry wine (4), or distilled (5) for brandy (6). Red grapes are trodden (9) and partly fermented (10) to make port (11). Brandy (5) is added to stop the process. The short fermentation and addition of brandy make the port sweet and strong.

Red grapes are crushed (1) and fermented in vats (2) to make red or rosé wines. To produce rosé (4) the juice is run off for further fermentation (3). Red wine is fermented for longer with the grape skins to obtain a deeper color, then left to ferment in barrels (5). This is known as 'free-run' wine. The skins are pressed (6) to make 'press wine' (7), which is sometimes added to the free-run wine to improve the quality. Any remaining stems or skins, the marc (8), are distilled for low grade brandy or are simply used to fertilize the land.

flavor possible. This process will occur more or less frequently, although this does depend on the individual wine. The residue is pressed and the wine is pumped to settling tanks. After several days, the clear wine is drawn off and the sediment discarded. The wine is then placed in large oak tanks to undergo a secondary fermentation. This process transforms malic acid into lactic acid and is encouraged by bacteria rather than yeasts. The secondary fermentation allows the wine to develop a softness and gives it the potential for complexity and finish. Once the malolactic fermentation is complete, the wines are either blended or put straight away into smaller oak casks, where they are allowed to mature.

The best white wines are produced by much the same process, with a couple of important variations. First, the skins and seeds are pressed with the grapes and then discarded. Since most color comes from these "impedimenta" it is necessary to remove them to keep the wine clear and pristine. The premium wines are made from first pressings only, secondary and tertiary pressings being consigned to inferior wines. The clear juice is allowed to settle, to rid it of solids and pulp, and the result is then drawn off to a fermentation tank. After one or two weeks at a temperature of 50 to 60 degrees Fahrenheit, the fermentation is complete and the wine is then either pumped to storage tanks or laid down in small barrels for aging, though the process is never as long as with red wines. Most whites are bottled within a year.

What we have described is the basic technique of winemaking, but many other factors enter into the production of a fine wine. One of the annoying peculiarities of wine is that, if exposed to air, it will turn to vinegar. Another, not so annoying, phenomenon, is that if kept in wood barrels, which act as dense membranes, wine can breathe very gently and improve dramatically. Through a millenium of experimentation it was discovered that oak, especially that of Limousin in France and from certain areas of Germany, would impart its own unique flavor to wine. Thus the barrel plays a vital role in the making of fine wines.

However the majority of table wine is not aged in barrels. It would be far too expensive and time-consuming. But for any wine that is meant to be savored rather than gulped, those months or years in wood can make the difference between a sound, ordinary wine and a great vintage. The size of that barrel also makes a big difference. Smaller barrels are used for fine reds, as they allow for more wood in contact with a given volume of wine and a greater impartation of the oak tannins and other flavor-enhancers. Larger barrels are used for lighter wines and for those whites that will improve with barrel aging. In general, white wines are not given the same lengthy time in barrels as are reds, since their freshness and fruitiness would be lost to the wood.

As the wine settles in wood, it is racked or transferred to clean barrels, and any sediment is drawn off. Red wines are also fined, much like clarifying a consommé. Egg white, which carries sediment and solid matter to the bottom of the cask, is used for this clarifying. White wines are also fined, though somewhat differently. Fine clay, which reacts with the proteins in the wine, are used to promote clarity. Needless to say, evaporation plays a role in barrel aging too. It is necessary to top-up each barrel periodically by hand to avoid any direct contact of the wine therein with air.

Bottling, though simple, demands extreme care. All the components, including machines, bottles and corks, must be carefully sterilized. The wine is run from tank or cask through a final filter — in the case of ordinary wines — and then most gently into the bottles. A vacuum is created in the neck and the cork is thrust home. All that needs be done is to compress a capsule over the cork and attach a label on the side. Then, depending on the quality of the wine, it can be laid down to age for a year or two or more. With luck, you will have a splendid wine as a result of all these processes combined with the care and art of the winemaker.

WINE AND FOOD

The pleasures of the table are the most constant of all. One can tire of many things, but eating and drinking have held sway since the dawn of human appreciation. Imagine, if you will, a perfect roast chicken, plain and simple, gently basted with tarragon and the best butter, wafting its seductive aroma across the table. What nectar should each forkful be allowed to share? The old standard rule of red meat/red wine, white meat/white wine was an English dictum, developed in those days of gargantuan banquets, where sauces were brown or white, and roasts came in full-animal sizes. Eating habits have changed more than a little over the past 100 years, especially in America. No longer soup, fish, meat, dessert, savory. No longer two or three wines with dinner. No longer a formal reverence for the eventual contents of the stomach, usually without regard to taste. Today, people are more willing to try unexpected wines with their food.

We do not mean to imply that anything goes. However, certain traditional combinations are best ignored if your tastebuds encourage you to do so, but experiment you must. One of us likes Madeira with smoked salmon, despite the constant dictum that you should *always* drink a very dry white wine with it. But at the other end of the spectrum is the school of wine appreciation, best practiced by the British, that says you *must* drink a Burgundy with game, a Bordeaux with lamb, a Muscadet with oysters and a Puligny-Montrachet with poached St. Pierre. Frankly, we feel that, despite a basic good sense of proportion, this is most untrue, especially for the current American way of doing things. We believe that America has finally begun to discover its culinary self. No more the slavish reliance on things and tastes European. We produce food and wine equal to almost anything in the world. What we do not produce are enough people who care about the preparation of our good raw materials.

Nevertheless, we are beginning to rediscover our culinary heritages, and our regional cuisines are aided — and sometimes hindered — by a flurry of new magazines devoted to the glossier pleasures of the table. Radio and TV commentators sing the praises of this wine or that cassoulet, but let us start with a few basics about what wine should accompany what food:

Beef and lamb, red wine.
Chicken, red or white, depending on the sauce.
Turkey and duck, red or white.
Pork, we prefer white.
Fish, generally white, dry.

Shellfish, fuller white, though exceptions exist.
Eggs, light fruity red.
Desserts, sweet white.
Appetizers, usually a white champagne-type.
Pasta, dependent on sauce.

Obviously these are reasonable suggestions, but what of the exceptions? Virtually no beef or lamb dishes taste like much of anything with white wine, and vice versa. Lamb, one of our favorite meats, needs a full, characterful red to do it justice and to stand up against the herbs and garlic that make it so good. Beef needs a truly powerful red, a Cabernet or Merlot or powerful Zinfandel. Pork is, as Grimod de la Reynière put it, the most encyclopedic of animals. A roast loin of pork with truffles can glory in a bottle of aged Cabernet, but spare-ribs would do better with a cheap generic red. Personally, we prefer a not-too-dry white with most pork, something to both complement and cut the richness of this very fatty meat. Ham, if it is good, and aged country hams can take a really rich white wine, a good Riesling or Gewürztraminer or Sauvignon Blanc.

Despite the usual blather about white wine with fish — the better the fish, the better the white, for instance — certain preparations of fish, and for that matter certain types, actually go well with a not-too-heavy red. Salmon, carp, bluefish, fresh tuna and other rather oily fish can often overpower even the strongest white wines. Unlike those in the south of France, American vintners have not seen fit to produce the honey-rich whites of the Jura, which go so well with fish.

Mollusks *do* taste better with white wines, but crustaceans are a mixed bag. Crabs and shrimps are delicate creatures. Lobster can stand up to a Zinfandel or a light Merlot. Most cooks have a tendency to overzealously decorate crustaceans with sauces, but if these creatures are just gently cooked and prettily served, nothing complements them better than the best dry white wine you can afford. A top Chardonnay, the equivalent of a great white Burgundy (a Montrachet), is the best choice. Failing that, try a Chenin Blanc or Sauvignon Blanc.

To start the meal we would choose a light white or an extremely dry sparkling wine. An alternative would be a very dry sherry or other fortified wine. Anything sweet will kill the appetite. The idea of an aperitif is to cleanse the palate, not to give one a sticky tongue. If the appetizers are to be rough and ready — cold cuts, a *salade niçoise* — even a light red would not be out of place. Of course, one would not expect lobster with vanilla à la Senderens after this fare. The main course might be an omelette and a salad. And here we come to the two of three exceptions to wine drinking. Eggs are nourishing, tasty and light. They have little affinity to wine and so you should not waste anything very good on them. With salads no wine is the best choice, as the acid components of virtually all salad dressings will make *any* wine taste awful!

Despite the clarion call of French restaurants that wine is perfect with cheese, we cannot agree. Most cheeses overpower anything but the strongest of red wines. Finish what you have in your glass, by all means, but never open a bottle especially for the cheese.

Desserts are another matter. The light pastries of good Italian or French patissiers can act as an admirable accompaniment to sweet dessert wines. But in America, where cakes and cookies are rich and often chocolate-flavored, or nut-encrusted and iced, better a good glass of brandy or other astringent liquor. Any fine sweet wine will be lost when put up against such competition.

The ordinary wine is for everyday, the great wine for great days — feasts, celebrations, and so on. You will inevitably disagree with us if you pursue your interest in wine. Fine. We have stated what we like, but we lay down no rules, and hope you will not either. Too many wine snobs flaunt their hidebound "knowledge" and we would never wish to add to their number.

WINE TASTING

Tasting wine is more than merely drinking it. Wine is one of the few relatively harmless pleasures left in this world, and on a scale rating, one of the least expensive for the amount of satisfaction. Good wine is "tasted" by sight, smell and touch, as well as taste.

After you have opened a bottle, let it sit for a few moments to dispel the odor of cork. If it is a young wine, leave it opened for an hour in a dark place. . . the wine will be able to breathe and perhaps soften. After pouring a glass hold it up to the light. Your search is for a pleasing color and clarity. Every wine is slightly different in hue, from deep purple-reds to crimsons to the color of maroon lacquer. Whites can vary from almost olivy greens to clear amber to the color of old gold. Part of the pleasure of fine wine is that the look of it whets the appetite, heightens the senses and prepares one for a whiff of magic.

That whiff or inhalation is made up of two distinct items: aroma, the scent of the grape, and bouquet, a more complex odor that develops from chemical changes the wine undergoes naturally as it ages. The best way to appreciate the smell of wine is to inhale for a few seconds and then give your nose a rest. The nose tires easily, and a series of scents will totally disorient it in no time at all. You should look for a vinous smell, one that resembles wine not grape juice; a clean quality, devoid of ungainly odors . . . rottenness, cork, mold; and occasionally, an odor other than the grape but related to particular grapes. . . a fruitiness of raspberries, or a spiciness like nutmeg, or nuttiness.

Finally — and like all sensible connoisseurs you are beginning to pant for a taste — let the wine roll over your lips and your tongue before swallowing. Note the tartness, sweetness, bitterness and body. Each plays a role in tasting wine, and each in varying combinations makes for pleasure or repugnance, memorability or boredom. Usually, though not always, a drier wine will be more complex to taste than a sweeter one. The great sweet wines of the Rhine are exceptions and Tokai Aszu from Hungary is another. The final lingering taste, or "finish", is what really sets a great wine apart from a merely good one. The body of a wine informs the mouth of its wateriness or hotness against the palate. Heavy and light are other informed terms used to describe body, and after a little practice, you should have no trouble recognizing either. Balance is the thing to look for last. A light, well-balanced wine may be preferable to a grand, vibrant, pure varietal. In fact, one of the more ill-conceived trends in California viticulture in the 1970s was the tendency among certain winemakers to produce astoundingly strong wines that overpowered almost every palate they rolled over. Balance is really the sum of all the constituent *perceived* qualities of a wine. They must react with one another with harmony. The senses should glow.

BELOW *Robert Mondavi inhales the aroma and bouquet of the wine, which will be a guide to its quality.*

Very few palates are distinct or unique. All can be trained to distinguish and appreciate good wines. Practice and keep notes of your tastings for future reference. Should you wish to organize a wine-tasting for your friends or colleagues, there is little to prepare, except remember to shun the usual wine and cheese party. As we have already mentioned, very few wines can stand up to the powers of most cheeses, and blander foods are better accompaniments to good wine. If you are drinking red wine, open plenty of bottles before your guests arrive so that the wine has a chance to breathe. Make sure that white wine is well chilled but not too cold to drink. Most important, you should check that plenty of glasses are at hand. Do not chill glasses for white wine — it dulls the senses and hurts the lips! For the accompaniment have olives (not too salty), cold chicken (at room temperature), mild vegetables, good poached fish, and plenty of crusty bread. Stay away from garlic, vinegar, lemons, fruits, deli meats and pretension. Above all, keep the ceremony in moderation, as everything else. The best way to appreciate wine is to enjoy it with good food and good fellowship.

THE WINES OF
CALIFORNIA

The wine industry in California since the mid-1960s has been in a period of rapid improvement and growth. New wineries spring up constantly and old ones change hands which makes it hard to generalize about regions. The discussion below is only a guide. The state of California is some 700 miles long, stretching from north to south along the Pacific Ocean. It covers a wide range of microclimates on latitudes comparable to all the major winemaking regions of Europe, from the cool Rhine to the heat of North Africa.

—NORTH COAST COUNTIES—

In the north of the state is the region called the North Coast Counties. This area includes vineyards in Lake County, Mendocino, the Napa Valley and Sonoma.

Lake County Lake County is inland, north of Mendocino and Napa. It is a fairly new area, but has already become well known for Rieslings.

Mendocino In the mountainous region north of Napa, Mendocino County is the home of Fetzer, Cresta Blanca and Parducci wineries.

Napa Valley The Napa Valley is some 35 miles long. It begins in the north near Calistoga and runs south to the town of Napa. Some of the vineyards found in the warmer northern area are Cuvaison, Sterling and Chateau Montelena. Moving south to the St. Helena area, the notable vineyards are too numerous to mention. Further south is the famed Stag's Leap area. Among the vineyards found here are Inglenook, Grgich Hills, Robert Mondavi and Clos du Val. Carneros Creek is at the southern end of the valley.

Sonoma Sonoma County, west of the Napa Valley and bordered by the Pacific, includes the Alexander, Dry Creek, Russian River and Bennett Valleys. Vineyards such as

Trentadue, Preston and Souverain are found there. Further south is Santa Rosa. Among others in this area are Iron Horse Vineyards, Dehlinger Winery and Glen Ellen Vineyards. In the southernmost part is Sonoma, home of Sebastiani, Hacienda and Buena Vista.

SAN JOAQUIN VALLEY

East of San Francisco Bay is the San Joaquin Valley. This region with its hot climate is home to some of the giant wine producers, including Gallo. The major towns are Lodi, Bakersfield and Fresno.

CENTRAL COAST COUNTIES

To the south and east of San Francisco are the Central Coast Counties, including Monterey, Santa Barbara County and the Santa Cruz Mountains.

Alameda Alameda County, or Livermore Valley, is southeast of San Francisco. Among the vineyards in this area are Concannon, Wente Brothers and Richard Carey Winery.

Amador Some memorable place-names are in Amador County, including Fiddletown, Placerville and Sutter Creek. The area is in the foothills of the Sierras east of Sacramento.

Monterey South of San Francisco, Monterey is a fairly new wine region. The Paul Masson Pinnacles Vineyard and Chalone Vineyard are found here.

San Benito Almost all the vineyards in the San Benito County are owned by either Almadén or Cienega. The major town is Hollister.

San Luis Obispo Some new vineyards show promise in San Luis Obispo County, notably the Hoffman Mountain Ranch. The area is quite far south of San Francisco.

Santa Barbara The area is in the foothills of the Sierra Madre Mountains, and includes the Santa Ynez Valley. Among the vineyards here are Sanford & Benedict, Firestone and Zaca Mesa.

Santa Clara The Santa Clara region was once a thriving winemaking area, until encroaching development took over many vineyards in the 1950s and 1960s. Some major wineries remain, including Mirassou, Martin Ray and David Bruce.

Santa Cruz The lush mountainous area north of the town of Santa Cruz has several wineries, including Bargetto, Ahlgren, Staiger and Roudon-Smith.

TEMECULA

In the far south of California is a microclimate near San Diego known as Temecula. The best known vineyard in this region is Callaway.

BELOW LEFT *The young grape needs plenty of rain and no frost. The vintner must carefully decide when the grapes are ripe for harvesting* (MAIN PICTURE). *Picked too soon they will lack enough sugar for fermentation, but left too late means they will absorb excess moisture and start to go moldy* (BELOW RIGHT).

ACACIA WINERY

Acacia Winery was founded in 1979 to produce only the Burgundian varietals, Pinot Noir and Chardonnay, from grapes grown in the Carneros district of southern Napa Valley. The philosophy of production at Acacia combines modern California technology with traditional Burgundian winemaking techniques. The Pinot Noirs, for example, are fined but not filtered. Managing partners Michael Richmond and Jerry Goldstein place enormous emphasis on the unique nature of the individual vineyards that provide fruit to Acacia. The vineyards, all within a mile of each other in Carneros, are designated on the labels. Marina Vineyards for example is estate-owned, planted exclusively in Chardonnay.

Few wines have been released yet by Acacia, but one of the best available is Chardonnay.

AHLGREN VINEYARD

Definitely a personal winery reflecting the interests of its owners, Ahlgren Vineyard was founded in 1976 by Dexter and Valerie Ahlgren. The winery is tucked into the north slope of the hillside beneath their mountain home in the northeastern area of Santa Cruz County. The Ahlgrens produce small amounts of wine using traditional techniques. Most of their grapes are purchased from the finest wine-growing regions, including the Napa and Livermore Valleys, but some of their Chardonnay is from their own planting.

Ahlgren Vineyard wines have won some important awards, including gold medals for Cabernet Sauvignon and Chardonnay at Los Angeles County Fairs. Interestingly, the Cabernet was the top winner of the 1982 New York comparative tasting of 1978 French Bordeaux and 1978 California Cabernets. Ahlgren also makes premium Zinfandel and Semillon. The Zinfandel is unfined and unfiltered; it is well-balanced and spicy. The Semillon is barrel-fermented using Santa Cruz Mountains grapes. It is dry, delicate and fruity.

ALEXANDER VALLEY VINEYARDS

In 1842, Cyrus Alexander settled in the southeastern area of the Sonoma County Valley that now bears his name. The Wetzel family purchased the property in 1963 from the heirs of Alexander's granddaughter. They started planting vines the next year and had 240 acres by 1973. In 1975, the first estate-bottled Alexander Valley Vineyards wines were produced. Immediate critical acceptance and awards followed and have continued ever since.

Alexander Valley Vineyards produces only five wines. The 1980 Chardonnay is medium-heavy, mellow, buttery and intensely varietal; it won a gold medal at the 1982 Orange County Fair. The Cabernet Sauvignons are aged in barrels for 18 months and are very good. The Chenin Blancs are bone-dry and refreshing, as are the Chardonnays. Johannisberg Riesling is aromatic and wonderful as an aperitif. Also fine for that purpose are the Gewürztraminers, made in a light, less intense style. About 17,000 cases of wine are made each year and prices are quite reasonable.

The interior of Beaulieu Vineyard's contemporary Visitor's Center is adjacent to the winery in Rutherford, California, in the heart of the Napa Valley (LEFT). Beaulieu was founded in 1900 by Georges de Latour. The winery was instrumental in making the Napa Valley one of the world's leading wine regions. Up-to-date technology is used at the winery. Red wines are pumped from the bottom of open-topped stainless steel fermentation tanks and sprayed over the cap of skins and pulp that forms over the surface during fermentation (BELOW). This procedure, called pumping over, breaks up the cap and gives the wine a richer color and flavor. It also prevents the development of undesirable bacteria. In Beaulieu Vineyards Champagne cellar, the traditional hand-production operation known as the méthode champenoise takes place during secondary fermenation (RIGHT). This time-consuming operation produces carbonation within each bottle, which gives the wine its sparkle. Beaulieu Champagnes are available in limited quantities only.

ALMADEN VINEYARDS

A Burgundian named Charles Lefranc settled in the Santa Clara Valley in 1852, and with cuttings from his native France, established the first successful commercial vineyard in northern California. Lefranc became the founder of what was then called the New Almadén Vineyards, named after a quicksilver mine in the vicinity. Lefranc died in 1887; his son and heir died in 1909. The vineyard then sank into obscurity until 1941 when new owners revitalized it and purchased new vineyards. In 1967, Almadén was bought by the National Distillers and Chemical Corporation. Today, Almadén Vineyards is a vast operation producing more than 60 kinds of table, fortified and sparkling wines. The company owns outright 6,400 acres of prime vineyards; it controls 7,000 other acres, for a total of 15,300. The Cienega Winery near Hollister holds more than 37,000 small oak barrels — it is the world's largest wine cellar under one roof. The bottling line can produce 40,000 cases of still wine in a single day.

Rosé wine was first introduced to the United States by Almadén in 1942. The Grenache Rosé today is still the most popular rosé in the country. Starting in 1978, Almadén has produced a superpremium line called Charles Lefranc Founder's Wines. The Cabernet Sauvignon under this label is smooth and aromatic. The Zinfandel Royale has almost overwhelming fruitiness and bouquet, with high tannin and a deep purple hue. Other wines under this label include a fine Johannisberg Riesling, Chardonnay, Pinot St. George (a red wine from Monterey County grapes) and Fumé Blanc. A recent new venture for Almadén is producing Chardonnay with Laurent-Perrier, the famed French Champagne house. The wine is somewhat drier than most, with a higher acid content. Champagne-style wine from Almadén is good value. The Almadén Blanc de Blancs was served at President Reagan's inaugural.

Frenchman Charles LeFranc (TOP) *founded Almadén in 1852, making it the oldest producing winery in California. This* (ABOVE) *was a star attraction at the American Centennial in 1876 and 1976 Bicentennial.*

BARGETTO WINERY

The Bargetto family represents a winemaking heritage that began more than 300 years ago in the Piedmont region of Italy. The skills acquired there were brought to California by the brothers Phillip and John Bargeto. In 1933, after the repeal of Prohibition, they built the present winery along the banks of Soquel Creek in coastal Santa Cruz County. In the 1950s, the Bargettos began producing premium varietal wines.

In addition to award-winning Chardonnays and Rieslings, Bargeto makes a dry French Colombard and a medium-dry Chenin Blanc. Among Bargetto's fine red wines are Cabernet Sauvignon, Barbera in the traditional robust Italian style, Zinfandel, Petite Sirah and the subtly flavored Pinot Noir.

The 1981 Bargetto Chardonnay was made from Napa Valley grapes. Cold-fermented, completely dry and aged for six months in oak barrels, this delicate and aromatic wine is a classic example of today's California Chardonnays.

BEAULIEU VINEYARD

In the annals of California winemaking, the name Beaulieu stands out as remarkable. The vineyard was founded in 1900 by Georges de Latour, and quickly became one of the leading producers of fine wines in the Napa Valley. A great deal of Beaulieu's later success was due to the brilliant decision of de Latour to bring André Tchelistcheff to the winery in 1938. This legendary winemaker remained for 35 years, bringing Beaulieu wines to a high level of estate-bottled quality. Beaulieu Vineyard was purchased by Heublein, Inc. in 1969. Since then the annual production has risen sharply to over 200,000 cases. Grapes con-

tinue to come from the winery's vineyards in central Napa Valley, with some from its vineyards in the Carneros region of southern Napa.

Beaulieu produces an extensive range of varietal table wines, as well as sparkling wines, generics, and dessert and sherry wines. Limited selections of special reserve wines are labeled as Georges de Latour Founder's Wines. The Private Reserve Cabernet Sauvignon under this label is consistently superb. Other outstanding wines from Beaulieu include Pinot Noir, Pinot Chardonnay, dry Sauvignon Blanc, and Johannisberg Riesling. Beaulieu produces an uncommon Muscat de Frontignan, a fortified dessert wine made in limited quantities.

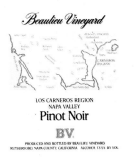

BELOW *Beaulieu Vineyard is located 60 miles north of San Francisco in the famed Napa Valley. The winery is open daily for tastings and tours.*

Chardonnay grapes (ABOVE) *are harvested at the Beaulieu vineyards in the Carneros region of the southern Napa Valley. The microclimate there is ideal for these grapes. The wine is made at the winery in Rutherford* (LEFT).

BOEGER WINERY

Boeger Winery and vineyards lie in the foothills of the Sierra Nevada range, just east of the historic town of Placerville, in El Dorado County's blossoming wine country. The family-owned winery was established in 1972 on the hillside terrain of a 70-acre ranch. Some vines and wine artifacts of the original winery, homesteaded in 1857, still remain on the site. Today, over 20 acres of premium grapes are in full production on the estate. More vineyard plantings are scheduled to bring annual production up to 10,000 cases.

Boeger Winery produces prize-winning varietal wines, all made from El Dorado County grapes. The 1979 Cabernet Sauvignon is dry with good acidity and should age well. Chardonnay from 1981 is mellow and rich, with varietal complexity; the 1981 Chenin Blanc is bone-dry and crisp, with a light body. Estate-bottled from high-grown grapes, the 1980 Merlot is spicy and intense, with a dark garnet color. Also estate-bottled is the 1981 Sauvignon Blanc, fruity and flowery. The 1980 Zinfandel is light-bodied, with spicy, peppery overtones.

Boeger makes blend wines: Sierra Blanc, Hangtown Gold and Hangtown Red. (During the Gold Rush era, Placerville was called Hangtown.)

DAVID BRUCE WINERY

Something of a controversial legend in California winemaking, Dr. David Bruce marketed his first wines in 1967. His 25-acre vineyard and winery are 2,000 feet up in the wooded Santa Cruz Mountains of Santa Cruz County; they produce 20,000 cases a year. As a protegé of Martin Ray, Bruce makes intense varietal wines that command rather a stiff price. He is also famous for his experiments, including making California's first white Zinfandel and being among the first to experiment with whole-berry fermentation.

A full range of varietal wines is produced at David Bruce Winery, but the primary interest is in Chardonnay and Pinot Noir. The estate-bottled Chardonnays are exceptionally fine — buttery, well-balanced and beautifully toasty.

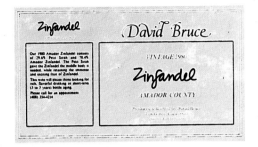

BUENA VISTA WINERY AND VINEYARDS

The father of California viticulture, Count Agoston Haraszthy, came to the Valley of the Moon in Sonoma County in 1857. He purchased the Buena Vista site and began expanding the estate, until the winery had over 400 acres of vineyards and was one of the leading wine producers in California. The vineyards survived phylloxera in the 1890s, but when the San Francisco earthquake of 1906 destroyed Buena Vista's storage tunnels, Haraszthy gave up. The estate vineyards were neglected until 1943, when they were replanted and winemaking resumed under the direction of Frank Bartholomew, who now owns Hacienda Wine Cellars. In 1968, new owners began planting additional vines, for a total acreage of 620. In 1979, the operation was sold to a German group, under whose control expansion and high quality continue. The capacity of the ultramodern winery is large. The bottling line can handle 1,500 cases per day, with storage for 900,000 and 300,000 gallons fermenting.

Buena Vista produces an extensive line of premium varietals. When exceptional wines are produced, they are labeled Special Selection. The 1979 Cabernet Sauvignon was deliberately made in a softer style for good drinkability now, but it will also age well. The 1980 Chardonnay is remarkable for its early maturity. It has a complex aroma and a full-bodied texture.

BURGESS CELLARS

ABOVE *The wine cellar at Burgess dates in part from around 1880. It is a careful blend of Old World stone architecture and modern winemaking equipment.*

Wine enthusiasts Tom and Linda Burgess founded Burgess Cellars in 1972. After considering several options, they chose the site of an existing winery and vineyard on the western slope of Howell Mountain, just northeast of St. Helena in the Napa Valley. Burgess Cellars specializes in only three varietals: Chardonnay, Zinfandel and Cabernet Sauvignon. Oak casks are used as fermenters for the Chardonnay — a rare technique that adds an unusual complexity. These wines have received many awards over the years, but their quantity and distribution are limited.

The 1979 Cabernet Sauvignon Vintage Selection was released in the spring of 1982. Deep in color and rich in aroma and taste, this superb wine will continue to gain complexity for up to 15 years with proper cellaring. Mountain-grown grapes were used to produce the 1980 Zinfandel and as a result the wine is intensely flavored and well-balanced, with a very long finish. The 1981 Chardonnay has a full aroma of ripe fruit, which is accompanied by the toasty flavor of French oak. This is a crisp, dry wine.

DAVIS BYNUM WINERY

In 1965, Davis Bynum quit the newspaper business to pursue his winemaking hobby on a full-time basis. He founded his winery in industrial Albany, California, but soon ran out of space there. The current winery, in an ultramodern former hop kiln in Sonoma County's Russian River Valley, was founded in 1973. Two-thirds of its grapes come from the area; the rest are from selected vineyards in Dry Creek and Alexander Valleys. The annual production is about 20,000 cases a year, chiefly in five major varietals. Smaller bottlings of other wines are sometimes made and sold at the winery only.

The 1975 and 1976 Davis Bynum Pinot Noirs are considered collector's items today. The 1979 bottling, just released, also promises great things for the future. Zinfandel from 1979 is exceptionally full-bodied, with high alcohol (13.9%) and deep

color. It should age remarkably well in the bottle. The reserve bottling of 1980 Chardonnay is a strong, dominant wine, while the Fumé Blanc from 1980 is flowery and elegant. Although the 1979 Cabernet Sauvignon lacks complexity, it is lively with rich varietal character.

CAKEBREAD CELLARS

Jack Cakebread founded this family vineyard in the heart of the Napa Valley in 1973. The original 22 acres of vineyard have recently been supplemented by a 12-acre block of Cabernet Sauvignon, but the Cakebreads must still purchase other grapes from growers in the Napa Valley. Annual production is about 25,000 cases of outstanding wine.

The 1979 Cabernet Sauvignon is powerful and complex; it has aged well, as have all the other Cakebread Cabernets. The varietal character of the 1980 Chardonnay comes out strongly to produce a wine that is simple and elegant. In contrast, the 1981 Sauvignon Blanc is highly complex, with the oak flavors well in the background. Cakebread Cellars also produces Zinfandel with an intense varietal flavor and zingy pepper taste; the 1979 and 1980 vintages are especially good.

BELOW *The winery and vineyards at Cakebread Cellars represent scientific winemaking at its best. The deep-water retrieval system, for example, was installed in 1973 and has become the model for all of the Napa Valley.*

CALERA WINE COMPANY

The world's first and only completely gravity-flow winery is found at Calera Wine Company in San Benito County. The recently completed winery is located on a steep slope; the must flows downhill from the presses to the fermentation vats and from there to the aging cellars which are further downhill.

Josh Jensen of Calera planted his three Pinot Noir vineyards — Selleck, Reed and Jensen — in 1975. That same year the first wine, a Zinfandel, was made from purchased grapes. Zinfandels were also made exclusively in 1976 and 1977, but starting with the 1978, Pinot Noirs and Zinfandels have been made every year. Jensen has recently begun a major commitment to Chardonnay as well. Current overall production has been increased to 8,000 cases a year.

The 1979 Pinot Noirs were released in the fall of 1981. The Selleck vineyard yielded a total production of only 111 cases of rich, full wine; Reed produced 84 cases with a very intense nose; and Jensen yielded 101 cases of complex wine with a very long aftertaste. The 1979 Zinfandels are available in much greater quantities — 1,450 cases of Templeton were made with an elegant, balanced taste and 1,188 cases of Doe Mill have a deep ruby color and strong aromas.

CALLAWAY VINEYARD & WINERY

The Temecula area, south of Los Angeles, is one of California's newest wine regions. The area is hot and arid, but cooled by winds from the Pacific Ocean that blow through the Rainbow Gap in the coastal mountain range. Callaway Vineyard and Winery is the main winemaker in the area. The vineyard of 140 acres was planted in 1969 and the first vintage was in 1974. Callaway was founded by Ely Callaway, the former head of Burlington Mills. Although he has recently sold his company to Hiram Walker, the giant distilling firm, Callaway continues to direct operations. The production has now climbed to over 65,000 cases a year, almost all of it in dry white varietal wines.

With rare exceptions, all Callaway wines are vintage-dated and estate-bottled. Chenin Blanc from Callaway is dry, with good color and balance. The 1980 and 1981 releases are excellent buys. The 1981 dry White Riesling has an almost smoky character, with a spicy aroma. Among the other whites are a full, melony 1981 Chardonnay, a fruity 1981 Sauvignon Blanc and a subtle 1981 Fumé Blanc. Perhaps the most interesting wine from Callaway is a late-harvest, botrytized Chenin Blanc called Sweet Nancy after Ely Callaway's wife. The deep golden color and sweet, fruity flavor are rich and full in the mouth, making this complex wine one of California's most unusual.

CARNEROS CREEK WINERY

The Carneros district is the coolest and southernmost viticultural area of the Napa Valley. The microclimate is near ideal for growing Pinot Noir and Chardonnay grapes. The primary goal of the well-known Carneros Creek Winery is the perfection of these two wine varieties, although the winery also produces Cabernet Sauvignon from the Napa Valley and Sauvignon Blanc from select vineyards in California.

Carneros Creek was founded in 1971, and has worked since then to establish long-term relationships with growers and to identify their vineyards on the wine labels. The winery is designed to handle an annual production of 15,000 cases all sold at a reasonable price.

Snow-capped mountains form the background to the Callaway vineyards in winter (MAIN PICTURE). This vine on an experimental plot has both Chenin Blanc and Zinfandel grapes growing on it. The bunches are in perfect condition, with berries of equal size (BELOW). Wines are made in the German style at Callaway. BOTTOM The stainless steel fermentation tanks are in the background, and German white oak barrels are in the foreground. Grapes are hand-harvested at the Callaway vineyards in Temecula, a new wine-growing region south of Los Angeles. The Rainbow Gap in the coastal mountain range (INSET RIGHT) allows cooling winds from the Pacific Ocean to blow over the area.

CASSAYRE-FORNI CELLARS

A partnership of two third-generation wine families, Cassayre-Forni Cellars was established in 1976. The partners, who own no vineyards, built their winery in 1979 in Rutherford in the heart of the Napa Valley. The present production capacity is limited to 4,000 cases a year, but the partners hope to expand to 12,000 cases soon.

Cassayre-Forni concentrates on three varietal wines: Napa Chenin Blanc, Cabernet Sauvignon and Sonoma Zinfandel. A Napa Chardonnay, produced in 1981, has not yet been released. The winery's Chenin Blanc is consistently among the best produced in California. Its varietal character is strongly expressed within an excellent fruit/acid balance. Cassayre-Forni's Zinfandel captures the regional character of the Dry Creek area in a wine that is well-balanced with considerable vanilla in the finish. The 1978 Cabernet Sauvignon was an outstanding vintage and the 1979 vintage nearly matched it.

ABOVE *Modeled after a typical French* cave, *the Chalone winery was built in 1973 with an extensive underground cellar capable of holding 600 barrels. Both the white and red wines are aged in 60-gallon French oak barrels.*

CHALONE VINEYARDS

The chalky limestone soil of the Gavilan Mountains is quite similar to that of the Champagne district of France. When this was pointed out to Will Silvear in 1919, he began planting grapes on his ranch in the shadow of Chalone Peak. The vineyards flourished, expanding over 40 acres. After Silvear's death in 1957, the vineyard changed hands; the first wines to bear the Chalone Vineyard label were produced in 1960. In 1965, Richard Graff took over the operation and he has run it very successfully ever since. The first vintage to be marketed, and the one that brought the Chalone Vinyard wines to the attention of the wine-drinking public, was the great one of 1969. About 1,000 cases were produced. Richard Graff was joined in 1970 by Philip Woodward. Since then Chalone Vineyard has developed to its present size of 125 acres of vineyards and a winery producing 12,000 cases a year. It is one of the best-regarded vineyards in the country.

Chalone Vineyard grows, produces and bottles four superb estate-bottled wines: Chardonnay, Pinot Noir, Pinot Blanc and Chenin Blanc. The wines are produced in the classical Burgundian tradition, using oak barrels imported from one of Burgundy's finest coopers.

The vineyards and winery are located in Monterey County, approximately 1,500 feet above the Salinas Valley floor. The viticultural area has been designated as Chalone by the federal government in recognition of its unique grape-growing characteristics.

CHATEAU BOUCHAINE

The first wines from the new Chateau Bouchaine winery are scheduled for release in the spring of 1984. The winery is located in a renovated facility in the Carneros District of the Napa Valley and was founded in 1980. The surrounding 30 acres are planted only in Chardonnay vines. Chateau Bouchaine expects to produce 25,000 cases annually of elegantly styled premium wines, primarily Chardonnay and Pinot Noir.

It is too soon to tell what will happen at Chateau Bouchaine, but the indications are good. Look for the 1981 Winery Lake Pinot Noir, 1982 Napa Valley Chardonnay and 1982 Alexander Valley Chardonnay when they are released.

CHATEAU MONTELENA

Secluded in the wooded northern edge of the Napa Valley, this magnificent French chateau takes its name from nearby Mount St. Helena. Chateau Montelena was founded in 1882, but the vineyards fell into disuse during Prohibition. The current owners began operations in 1972, and achieved renown almost immediately. Their first wine, the 1972 Johannisberg Riesling, won the prestigious *Los Angeles Times* "Golden Eagle" award in 1972. In 1976, as a result of the now-famous "Paris Tasting," Chateau Montelena's 1972 Chardonnay was awarded first place over nine other first-rate French white Burgundies and California Chardonnays in a blind tasting. The Chardonnays are still first-rate, with a distinctive character and a faint hint of oak. Chateau

Montelena also makes a unique style of Zinfandel that is spicy, zesty and deep-colored. The Johannisberg Rieslings are cold fermented for five weeks, resulting in a delicate, fragrant nose and fruity flavors. The estate-bottled Cabernet Sauvignons are aged for two years in Nevers oak barrels and for an additional year in the bottle before release. The result is an intense Cabernet aroma with great depth of flavor.

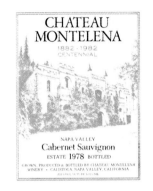

The estate building at Chateau Montelena is medieval in style (BELOW). Parts of it go back to 1882. The grounds also have Chinese gardens and summerhouse.

CALIFORNIA

LEFT *This is the Chalone Vineyard, which stretches for 125 miles in the Gavilan Mountain region. An area with superb vine growing conditions, it is similar to that of the Champagne district of France. The Chalone Vineyard tends to pour the grapes from their boxes straight into the fermenter tank without putting them through rollers (INSET). They also have their own design of hydraulic press to pack them down.*

BELOW *These Chinese-style gardens provide the setting for Chateau Montelena. During Prohibition the property was owned by a Chinese couple, the Yort Franks, who designed the grounds. The house itself is in medieval style.*

Chateau St. Jean Vineyards and Winery

In the short time it has been in operation, Chateau St. Jean has made its presence felt on the California wine scene. Chateau St. Jean was first conceived in 1973 by Ken Sheffield and Bob and Edward Merzoian. The three were already involved in the production of California table grapes and, as lovers of fine wines, wanted to get more involved with the fruit of the "other" grape.

All the people at Chateau St. Jean are firm believers in the subtle differences the varying microclimates and subsoils can make in a wine. They mix grapes from different vineyards only when the resulting wine is better than each vineyard would produce alone. Usually the grapes are crushed, fermented and aged separately; the wine is then bottled with the vineyard of origin shown on the label. Almost 90 percent of Chateau St. Jean's wines are in these small, defined lots.

The wines are all fermented in stainless steel with the exception of Chardonnay and Pinot Blanc. These start in steel, but are later transferred to traditional oak to finish fermenting and for aging. The Johannisberg Riesling, Gewürztraminer and Sauvignon Blanc are kept in stainless steel until bottling and, as a result, are very fresh, fruity wines.

The Christian Brothers

The century-old winemaking business of The Christian Brothers of California has been nurtured and perpetuated to assist the Order's educational and religious endeavors in the San Francisco Province. Since they began making wine in the Napa Valley in 1882, the Christian Brothers have acquired extensive properties in the Napa and San Joaquin Valleys. They now hold over 1,500 acres of prime vineyards, and produce a complete line of generic and varietal table wines, vermouths, champagne-style, dessert and aperitif wines, and brandy. The Brothers also produce highly respected sacramental wines. The internationally known cellarmaster at The Christian Brothers, Brother Timothy, has been actively involved with the vineyards and cellars since 1935.

The Christian Brothers wines are known for offering quality at a reasonable price. Particularly good values are the Cabernet Sauvignon and dry Chardonnay. The Grey Riesling, Gamay-Noir, Pinot Noir, Gewürztraminer and Napa Fumé Blanc are all worth investigating.

Clos du Bois

Like many other winemakers, Frank Woods started out as a grower. The first vineyards at Clos du Bois were planted in the Dry Creek Valley of Sonoma County in 1964. In subsequent years, Clos du Bois acquired property and planted vineyards in the adjacent Alexander Valley; in total, nearly 300 acres of prime varietal wines are now under cultivation. Winemaking began at Clos du Bois in 1974. From the start, the wines, produced in the French tradition, have been successful. Production has gradually grown until it now approaches 50,000 cases a year.

In recent years, Clos du Bois has begun producing "Vineyard Designation" wines. A particularly interesting one is the Marlstone label, used for a Cabernet/Merlot blend from the Alexander Valley. The first release, from 1978, combines the rich flavors and dark purple hue of the Merlot with the peppery, herbaceous nose of the Cabernet in nearly equal proportions. Another outstanding wine is the Calcaire Chardonnay, also from the Alexander Valley. The 1979 release has an apple-vanilla flintiness, with a long, clean finish. Clos du Bois makes a full range of varietals including award-winning Gewürztraminers.

CLOS DU VAL

The wines of Clos du Val have a distinctly French style, the result of winemaker/owner Bernard Portet's French heritage. After arriving in America from France, Portet planted 120 acres of vines in the southeastern Napa Valley in 1972. His philosophy is to combine modern American technology with the best traditional methods of the French Medoc region in his winemaking. Clos du Val Cabernet Sauvignons, following the Medoc tradition, are made with a blend of Cabernet Sauvignon and Merlot wines, giving the result an amazing roundness, softness and complexity. The varietal Merlot from Clos du Val is also of the highest quality. Very round, it is full, soft and deep, with a lingering finish in the best French style. A very fruity and elegant Chardonnay has been produced since 1978.

Interestingly, it is with the uniquely American grape, Zinfandel, that Clos du Val has made its fame. Bordeaux techniques applied to these grapes create a wine that has all the freshness, fruitiness and roundness that Zinfandel is capable of producing.

BELOW *The barrel aging room at Clos du Val is where the flavor of the wood infuses into the wine to give it greater depth. This is especially important for red wines.*

COLONY WINES

Founded in 1881 as Italian Swiss Colony Winery, Colony Wines is run by Edmund A. Rossi, Jr., the grandson of the original winemaker. The winery is located in northern Sonoma County at Asti, 90 miles north of San Francisco. The winery has always been a large, successful operation producing mostly jug and generic wines. In 1981, however, Colony introduced a quality line of premium varietals.

Cabernet Sauvignon from Colony is full-bodied and made from a blend of several vintages. The Zinfandel has typical varietal characteristics and a good balance of acid and tannin. Chenin Blanc is aromatic and well-balanced; French Colombard is fresh and fruity with a crisp, clean taste.

CONCANNON VINEYARDS

In 1883, on the advice of Bishop Alemany of San Francisco, James Concannon planted 250 acres of prime European vines in the Livermore Valley. From the first, the wines were successful — the vineyards flourished, supplying cuttings from the noble varieties to many other California vineyards. Under James's son, "Captain Joe" Concannon, the winery survived the rigors of Prohibition, largely by making sacramental wine and selling grapes for the home market. Today, Jim Concannon, grandson of the founder, continues the family tradition of high-quality, reasonably priced table wines.

In 1965 Concannon bottled the first varietally-labeled Petite Sirah; it has since become one of the winery's most sought-after red wines. Sauvignon Blanc, a variety that is ideally suited to the climate and soil of the Livermore region, has always been one of Concannon's specialities. Other featured white varieties are Chardonnay, Johannisberg Riesling and Semillon. They also

LEFT *The Mediterranean-style building of the Chateau St. Jean Vineyard is situated at the foot of Sugarloaf Ridge. The dejuicing tanks* (INSET LEFT) *are where the juice is drawn off and the residue emptied into the pneumatic press* (INSET RIGHT). *This gently presses more juice from the sediment, which may be mixed with the wine later, depending on its quality. Most of the white wines at Chateau St. Jean are fermented in stainless steel containers* (ABOVE) *and then transferred to oak barrels to complete the process. French oak is used for Chardonnay. This is to give the wine a special, individual flavor.*

market a blended wine labeled Livermore Riesling, which is predominantly Johannisberg Riesling, along with Chenin Blanc, Colombard and Muscat Blanc. Recently, Concannon has begun a program of premium, estate-bottled wines that promises well for the future.

CONGRESS SPRINGS VINEYARDS

When Dan and Robin Gehrs began production at Congress Springs Vineyards in 1976, the result was a grand total of six barrels of wine. Since then, they have learned much and annual production now totals about 5,000 cases. The Gehrs use only grapes from small vineyards on the eastern slopes of the Santa Cruz Mountains to make their award-winning varietals.

The 1981 Fumé Blanc is made from grapes grown at the Alma Vineyard. Well-crafted and elegant, its fruit is well balanced by moderate acidity and a touch of oak. The distinguished line of Congress Springs Pinot Blancs continues with the 1981 release. Cabernet Sauvignon from Congress Springs is distinctively lighter than most. The Chardonnay from the Montmartre Vineyard has a remarkable range of flavors, despite coming from a very young vineyard. Although not botrytized, the 1980 late harvest Semillon is crisp, with a strong varietal flavor. Pinot Noir from 1979 has an earthy complexity; it should age well. Congress Springs also produces Zinfandel.

BELOW *Inside the Mediterranean-style villa is the winery at Congress Springs. The villa, built of solid concrete in 1923, is in the redwood-forested Santa Cruz Mountains.*

CRESTA BLANCA WINERY

Founded just over a century ago by Charles Wetmore, Cresta Blanca Winery produced the first California wine to win an international competition. Two Cresta Blanca wines won the coveted Grand Prix of the Paris Exposition in 1889 against 17,000 entrants. Today, a reproduction of the Grand Prix medallion appears on the label of every Cresta Blanca wine — of which there are many. The winery at Ukiah in Mendocino County produces 17 table wines, four dessert wines, three champagnes, and America's only vintage-dated brandy. The modern winery has a bottling line that can process 55 bottles a minute; storage capacity is over 500,000 gallons.

Of the table wines from Cresta Blanca, Zinfandel and Chenin Blanc won silver medals at the 1982 Orange County Fair. The sparkling wine made entirely from Chardonnay grapes is recognized as one of the finest champagne-style wines produced in California.

BELOW *Expansion and remodeling of the Cresta Blanca winery have recently been completed. The bottling line can rinse, fill, cork and label 55 bottles in one minute.*

CUVAISON WINERY

In French, *cuvaison* means the frothy purple juice of grapes fermenting on the skins. The image of intense, alive wines that this evokes is an apt one. Cuvaison Winery was founded in 1970 as a small rustic operation producing a wide variety of varietal wines. In 1973, the year the state-of-the-art technical facility was built, the original partners sold the winery. The current owners have reduced the number of wines produced to three —

CUVAISON
1978
NAPA VALLEY
ZINFANDEL

ALCOHOL 14% BY VOLUME
PRODUCED & BOTTLED BY CUVAISON VINEYARD,
CALISTOGA, NAPA VALLEY, CALIFORNIA, U.S.A.

Chardonnay, Cabernet Sauvignon and Zinfandel. Since 1979, they have also been planting a 400-acre vineyard in the Carneros region of the Napa Valley.

Following fermentation, Cuvaison wines receive a minimum of handling. The Chardonnay is filtered only once; the Cabernet and Zinfandel are fined with egg whites to ensure clarity. Aging is in small French oak cooperage. Despite an annual production of only 20,000 cases, Cuvaison wines are sold in 45 states and 12 countries.

Releases from Cuvaison in 1982 include an elegant 1980 Napa Valley Chardonnay and a spicy 1978 Napa Valley Zinfandel. The 1979 Cabernet Sauvignon was blended with a small percentage of Merlot for softness and complexity and then aged in Nevers oak for 18 months.

DE LOACH VINEYARDS

The transition from vineyardist to winemaker is not always a successful one, but the De Loach family provides a good example of how to do it well. They have been growing grapes in Sonoma County since 1972, but did not release their first wines until 1980. Current production is about 22,000 cases of well-crafted, clean, authentic wines a year. In addition to Fumé Blanc, Chardonnay, Gewürztraminer, Pinot Noir and Zinfandel, the De Loaches produce a white Zinfandel. With a distinctive pink color and excellent varietal character, this new release is a fine substitute for white wine. It has been received with good reviews and has already won two important medals. The 1980 estate-bottled white Zinfandel won the gold medal at the 1981 Sonoma County Harvest Fair, and the 1981 estate-bottled vintage took a silver at the 1982 San Francisco Fair and Exposition. At the same fair, the De Loach 1980 Russian River Valley Chardonnay won a silver medal; the 1981 vintage won a gold medal at the 1982 Sonoma County Harvest Fair.

DE LOACH
VINEYARDS

ESTATE BOTTLED
SONOMA COUNTY

WHITE ZINFANDEL
1981

PRODUCED & BOTTLED BY CECIL DE LOACH VINEYARDS
SANTA ROSA, SONOMA COUNTY, CALIFORNIA
ALCOHOL 12.0% BY VOLUME RESIDUAL SUGAR 1.1% BY WT.

BELOW *These great stainless steel vats are used to ferment champagne-type wines made at the Domain Chandon winery. Only the first pressing of the grapes is used for sparkling wines and any subsequent pressings are used for the winery's still varieties. The length of time the wines are kept in barrels varies considerably for each type. White wines are not generally left to age for as long as red wines. The Domain Chandon winery then bottles the wine and stores it in the endless lines of racks found in their cellars* (RIGHT) *for further fermentation.*

DIABLO VISTA WINERY

Benicia, in the Solano area of northern California on the Sacramento River, is not yet famous as a wine region. Nonetheless, the Diablo Vista Winery produces fine wines there, using grapes from its own vineyard in Sonoma County and also those from growers in Sonoma, the Napa Valley and the foothills of the High Sierras. The winery was established in 1977 and production is tiny — about 5,000 bottles a year, which rarely make it beyond stores in San Franciso and Sacramento.

Diablo Vista Zinfandel, made from its own grapes, is consistently fine, with good aroma and fruit. Chardonnay and Cabernet Sauvignon are also produced.

DIAMOND CREEK VINEYARDS

Diamond Creek is not one vineyard but three, all located within 20 acres on the northern face of Diamond Mountain, nearly 700 feet above the Napa Valley floor. Each vineyard distinctly varies in geological formation, and each produces a very different type of wine. Owner Al Brounstein planted his vines in 1968 and since 1972 has been growing, producing and bottling remarkable Cabernet Sauvignon — and nothing else. The wine is scarce — only 3,000 cases a year and is also expensive, but considered to be well worth it.

All Diamond Creek Cabernets are deep and intense, with a complex combination of strong fruits and tannins. They are aged for two years in Nevers oak before release. To the experienced taster, the differences between the vineyards are apparent. The wines from the Red Rock Terrace vineyard are soft and elegant, with a magnificent bouquet; those from Gravelly Meadow are lighter and pleasantly earthy. Volcanic Hill produces Cabernets that are mouth-filling and austere, with a powerful aroma.

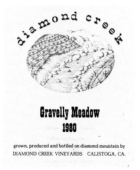

Gravelly Meadow
1980

grown, produced and bottled on diamond mountain by
DIAMOND CREEK VINEYARDS   CALISTOGA, CA.

DOMAINE CHANDON

After four years of development, Domaine Chandon offered its first sparkling wines in 1977. The winery is owned by the same French conglomerate that owns Champagne Moët et Chandon, makers of Dom Perignon Champagne. To control the winemaking process from start to finish, Domaine Chandon owns the 900-acre Carneros Ranch in the Napa Valley, along with a 200-acre vineyard on Mt. Veeder and a 130-acre vineyard surrounding the winery west of Yountville. The large, modern winery produces nearly 300,000 cases a year; production is projected to rise to 400,000 cases in the near future.

Domaine Chandon applies the traditional *méthode champenoise* to the creation of its sparkling wines. The Napa Valley Brut *cuvée* is generally two-thirds Pinot Noir and one-third Chardonnay with a small amount of Pinot Blanc. It has a classic champagne-style nose, coupled with the freshness and vigor of Napa Valley grapes. The Blanc de Noirs is a lightly tinted *oeil de perdrix* (eye of the partridge) sparkling wine made entirely from Napa Valley Pinot Noir grapes. It is fruitier and fuller-bodied than Napa Valley Brut. Domaine Chandon bottles its *tailles* (juice from the second and third pressings of the grapes) as still wine. Panache is Domaine Chandon's interpretation of a traditional Champagne region aperitif called ratafia. Fred's Friends Blanc Nature is a blend of the Chardonnay and Pinot Noir *tailles*. It is available only at the winery.

DRY CREEK VINEYARDS

About 70 miles north of San Francisco in the Dry Creek Valley of Sonoma County, Dry Creek Vineyard was founded in 1972. This small winery, owned by David Stare, originally a Bostonian, produces a maximum of 25,000 cases of varietal wines each year. The 50 acres of vineyard surrounding the winery are being developed. The vines yielded their first small crop in 1976; when mature, they should supply about half the winery's needs. The remainder of the grapes are purchased from a few quality-oriented growers in the Healdsburg/Dry Creek area. The wines at Dry Creek are given only a bare minimum of fining and filtering.

Dry Creek Fumé Blanc from 1981 has good varietal flavor, with a subtle hint of French oak aging and a characteristic grassiness. The 1981 Chenin Blanc is almost totally dry, with pleasing fruitiness. Fresh flavors and an elegant balance of wood and fruit characterize the 1981 Chardonnay. A good value from Dry Creek Vineyards is the 1979 Cabernet Sauvignon, which gives excellent balance at a reasonable price. The award-winning Zinfandel has moderate tannin with a classic, raspberry-like aroma.

DURNEY VINEYARD

Bill Durney, a fifth-generation Californian, and his wife Dorothy Kingsley, author of many screenplays for hit movie musicals, bought 1,200 acres of Carmel Valley land in 1954. Their plan, radical at the time, was to raise wine grapes. It was not until 1968, however, that the vines were planted and today the vineyard covers 116 acres. The annual yield has reached some 12,000 cases of estate-bottled wines.

The hallmark of Durney Vineyard is currently their 1979 Cabernet Sauvignon. It is aged in small oak barrels for 13 months, developing a dark color and a complex, mouth-filling flavor. In addition, Durney produces a unique, Carmel Valley Chenin Blanc and a lush Johannisberg Riesling. Their Gamay Beaujolais is very intense. It benefits well from cellaring but its supply is limited. However, those who have already discovered the wine from this vineyard hope it will increase in the future.

EDNA VALLEY VINEYARD

The winery of Edna Valley Vineyard is a joint venture of Chalone Vineyard, located in the Gavilan Mountains of Monterey County, and the Paragon Vineyard Company, within the Edna Valley in San Luis Obispo County. Producing only Chardonnay and Pinot Noir, this young company plans to release about 20,000 cases a year. The estate-bottled 1979 and 1980 Chardonnays, released in 1981 and 1982 respectively, have both been well received by the public. Toasty with an oaky aroma, these wines are a promising start for the vineyard. No Pinot Noirs have been released as yet, but the careful attention to detail shown so far in Edna Valley wines bodes well for the future. It is certainly one to watch.

FAR NIENTE WINERY

Far Niente takes its name from the Italian *dolce far niente*, or "without a care", given it in 1882 by founder John Benson. Far Niente flourished until the advent of Prohibition, when it and many others closed and were abandoned. After more than half a century of neglect, restoration at Far Niente was begun in the late 1970s by Gil Nickel and his partners, Doug Stelling and Bob Lieff. The art of winemaking returned to Far Niente in 1982. As part of the restoration, a cave was dug in the hill behind the winery. It is thought to be the first commercial wine cave built in the Napa Valley, and possibly in America, during this century. The Stelling Vineyard, consisting of 120 acres of Chardonnay and Cabernet Sauvignon vines, will eventually provide all the grapes for Far Niente wines. The winery has a maximum capacity of 22,000 cases; the annual production is currently 15,000.

Far Niente Chardonnay is produced exclusively from Napa Valley grapes. It is vinified in the traditional manner and aged in French oak to give a rich, full-bodied, yet delicate wine. The first release of Far Niente Cabernet Sauvignon is scheduled for 1985.

FETZER VINEYARDS

At the northern end of the California wine country, in Mendocino's Redwood Valley, is Fetzer Vineyards home ranch and winery. This family-owned and operated business was founded by Barney and Kathleen Fetzer and their 11 children in 1968; since their father's death in 1982, the children, led by the eldest brother John, continue in the family tradition. Fetzer Vineyards now produces over 250,000 cases of wine from the 168 acres of vines on the home ranch, and from selected vineyards in Mendocino and Lake Counties. Fetzer maintains completely separate wineries for red and white wines.

A full range of fine vintage-dated wines is made at Fetzer. Outstanding are the limited productions of special Zinfandels and Cabernets. There can be as many as six different bottlings of vineyard-designated Zinfandels in a vintage year; each is different, but all share the Fetzer style — full and firm. As with the Zinfandels, there are a variety of bottlings of Cabernet in each vintage, all with good structure and character.

ABOVE *Robert Fetzer in the 780-acre home vineyard in Redwood Valley, Mendocino County. Fetzer Vineyards is entirely owned and operated by 10 brothers and sisters.*

FIRESTONE VINEYARDS

The heir to one of the world's largest tiremakers, Brooks Firestone is totally dedicated to the quality of his winemaking. The first harvest from his 280 acres of vines in the Santa Ynez Valley was in 1975. All Firestone wines are grown, produced and bottled on the estate; the annual production is limited to 70,000 cases.

The first releases from Firestone were rosés. These are still made and they are generally light and refreshing. Cabernet Sauvignon from Firestone is velvety soft with exceptional bouquet; the 1977 vintage is excellent and fairly priced. Pinot Noir is in the Burgundian style and improves with each vintage, while the Merlot is rich and powerful. Among the white wines, Firestone Chardonnay is pleasantly fruity, with medium body and an oaky aroma. The Johannisberg Riesling has a distinctive varietal character and good acidity. The Selected Harvest from 1978 is a fine Riesling, with an intense, flowery bouquet. Gewürztraminer from Firestone is elegantly dry and good value.

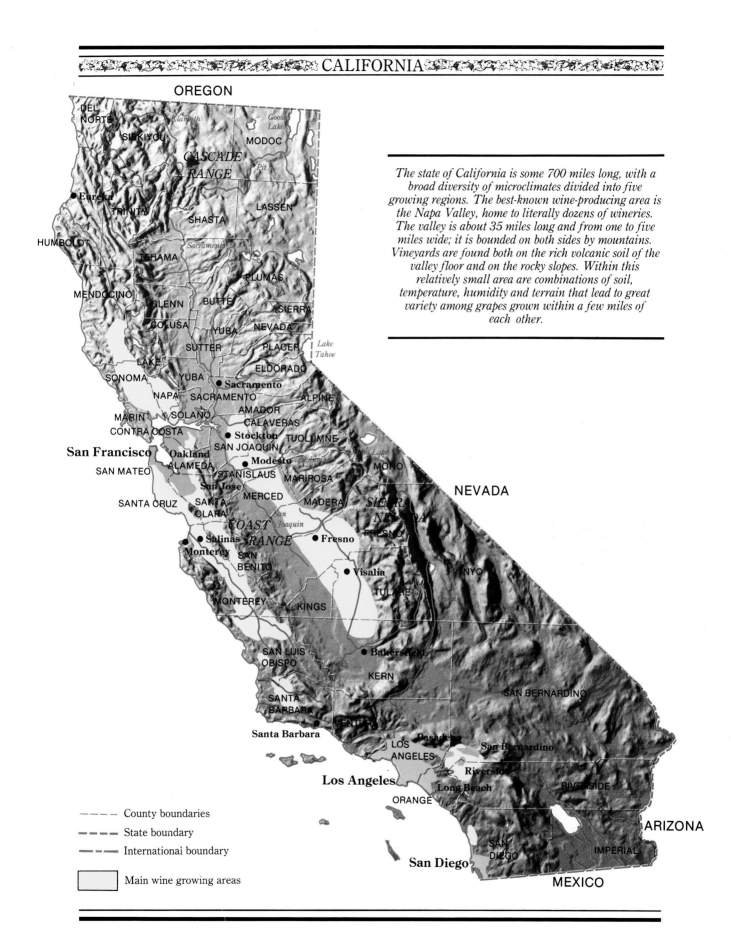

OREGON

DEL
NORTE

SISKIYOU

MODOC

*CASCADE
RANGE*

● Eureka

TRINITY

LASSEN

SHASTA

HUMBOLDT

TEHAMA

PLUMAS

MENDOCINO

GLENN

BUTTE

SIERRA

COLUSA

NEVADA

YUBA

LAKE

SUTTER

PLACER

Lake
Tahoe

ELDORADO

SONOMA

YUBA

NAPA

● Sacramento

SACRAMENTO

ALPINE

MARIN

SOLANO

AMADOR

CALAVERAS

CONTRA COSTA

● Stockton

TUOLUMNE

SAN JOAQUIN

San Francisco

Oakland

● Modesto

MONO

SAN MATEO

ALAMEDA

STANISLAUS

MARIPOSA

San Jose

SANTA CRUZ

SANTA
CLARA

MERCED

MADERA

*SIERRA
NEVADA*

*COAST
RANGE*

San
Joaquin

● Salinas

● Fresno

FRESNO

Monterey

SAN
BENITO

INYO

● Visalia

MONTEREY

TULARE

KINGS

NEVADA

SAN LUIS
OBISPO

● Bakersfield

KERN

SAN BERNARDINO

SANTA
BARBARA

VENTURA

Santa Barbara

Pasadena

San Bernardino

LOS
ANGELES

Riverside

Los Angeles

Long Beach

RIVERSIDE

ORANGE

ARIZONA

SAN
DIEGO

IMPERIAL

San Diego

MEXICO

- - - - - County boundaries
- - - - - State boundary
- - - - - International boundary

Main wine growing areas

The state of California is some 700 miles long, with a broad diversity of microclimates divided into five growing regions. The best-known wine-producing area is the Napa Valley, home to literally dozens of wineries. The valley is about 35 miles long and from one to five miles wide; it is bounded on both sides by mountains. Vineyards are found both on the rich volcanic soil of the valley floor and on the rocky slopes. Within this relatively small area are combinations of soil, temperature, humidity and terrain that lead to great variety among grapes grown within a few miles of each other.

FISHER VINEYARDS

Fisher Vineyards is situated high in the rugged Mayacamas Mountains that divide the Napa Valley from Sonoma County. The first vines were planted with Fred and Juelle Fisher in 1974; in 1982 they released their first Cabernet Sauvignon, from 1979, to excellent reviews. Their 1979 and 1980 Chardonnays, also well-received, are fully fermented in stainless steel and then aged in Limousin oak for eight months.

Because many of their vines are not yet fully mature, the Fishers purchase grapes from growers in the Dry Creek and Napa Valleys. However, they have recently completed the bottling of a small amount of their own 1980 Whitney's Vineyard Chardonnay. They have great hopes for this wine, and plan to make it into an annual estate bottling available at the winery.

FOPPIANO VINEYARDS

Owned, operated and managed by the Foppiano family, Foppiano Vineyards is one of the oldest in California. It is also one of the very few still owned and operated by the founding family. The first vineyard was planted by John Foppiano in 1896 at the Riverside Farm and wine was continually produced there until Prohibition. The family kept afloat during this bleak period by selling fresh grapes. Following Repeal, the winery was rebuilt and enlarged and business successfully resumed. In 1960 the Foppianos began planting premium varietal grapes; the vineyards now consist of approximately 200 acres along the Russian River in Sonoma County, planted in Cabernet Sauvignon, Sauvignon Blanc, Chardonnay, Pinot Noir, Merlot, Petite Sirah, Zinfandel and French Colombard. Some of the Zinfandel and Petite Sirah vines are over 70 years old and still producing. Grapes are also brought from many loyal growers in the area. Since 1979, excellent vintage-dated varietals have been released with the Louis J. Foppiano label; the less expensive wines are labeled just Foppiano. A new varietal label, Riverside Farm, has recently been approved for what the Foppianos call their "premium generics."

The capacity of the winery is about 1,000,000 gallons, which are stored in stainless steel vats, large redwood tanks and 50-gallon oak barrels. The fermenting room has stainless steel fermenting tanks that are capable of holding up to 75,000 gallons at any one time.

Riverside Farm
BY FOPPIANO

PREMIUM DRY ROSÉ
CALIFORNIA ROSÉ WINE

MADE AND BOTTLED BY L. FOPPIANO WINE CO.
HEALDSBURG/SONOMA COUNTY/CALIF./B.W. 312
ALCOHOL 12.5% BY VOLUME

FORTINO WINERY

Ernest Fortino's first exposure to winemaking came when he was six — treading the grapes in the family vineyard in Calabria, Italy. After his youth in Italy, Fortino studied enology in France and came to California in 1960. In 1970 he purchased an abandoned small bulk winery dating back to 1935, and Fortino Winery was born. The winery came into its own in 1977, when the Fortino entries collected eight medals — more than any other single winery at the Los Angeles County Wine Competition.

The Fortino vineyards now encompass a total of 65 acres planted in 10 varietals. About half the winery's grapes are grown on the estate, with the balance purchased from local Santa Clara Valley growers. The annual production is 15,000 cases, divided among some 24 different wines. Of particular interest are the Cabernet Sauvignon, distinguished by a smooth texture and clean bouquet, the Zinfandel Blanc, with a clear, fruity taste and the Petite Sirah, one of the finest wines to be produced in the region.

Fortino WINERY
California
ZINFANDEL BLANC
A UNIQUE CRISP ZINFANDEL GRAPE
(Serve Chilled)
ALCOHOL 12½% BY VOLUME
Produced and bottled by
FORTINO WINERY · SANTA CLARA COUNTY · GILROY, CA

Fortino WINERY
California
PETIT SYRAH
RICH, FULL-BODIED, VINTNER'S PRIDE
ALCOHOL 12½% BY VOLUME
Produced and bottled by
FORTINO WINERY · SANTA CLARA COUNTY · GILROY, CALIFORNIA

FRANCISCAN VINEYARDS

After a shaky start that saw several owners come and go, Franciscan Vineyards was purchased in 1979 by the German firm Peter Eckes. The winery has now settled down to producing high-quality varietal wines from its large vineyards in the Napa and Alexander Valleys. Although production has been cut back to concentrate on quality, more than 300,000 cases a year are produced. All vintage-dated wines labeled Alexander Valley, Napa Valley Estate Bottled and Private Reserve mean that they are produced from Franciscan's own vineyards.

Franciscan Vineyards is noted for its Cabernet Sauvignon. In addition to its routinely excellent releases of this wine, a Private Reserve Cabernet is made in selected years. The 1977 release is a good example. The Charbono from 1979 is a unique version of this rarely seen wine. Deep purple with a peppery nose and dry, full body, it is tart with good acid. Napa Valley Chardonnay from 1980 is clean, buttery and oaky; the 1981 Johannisberg Riesling is crisp and light, with an off-dry taste. An outstanding wine from Franciscan Vineyards is the 1981 Fumé Blanc. The label designation says merely California, but the taste is clean and delicate and the price is reasonable.

FREEMARK ABBEY WINERY

The first grapes were planted at the Freemark Abbey site in 1875 by William J. Sayward, a retired sea captain. In 1881, he sold his holdings to John and Josephine Tychson. John died soon after, but Josephine went on to build Tychson Winery in 1886, the first winery built by a woman in California. The property changed hands a number of times after phylloxera forced Josephine to sell her winery in 1894 and actually closed in 1965. Finally, in 1967, a group of partners reactivated the winery under the Freemark Abbey name. The partners later purchased the Red Barn Ranch in Rutherford in 1971; vine plantings there now cover 130 acres.

BELOW *The winery at Freemark Abbey was built in 1899 by the owner at the time, Anton Forni.*

The Freemark Abbey Chardonnay created a sensation when first released in 1969; its sweet golden Edelwein, made from botrytized grapes, created another when first released in 1973. In addition to these wines, Freemark Abbey also produces excellent Johannisberg Rieslings, Cabernet Sauvignons and Petite Sirahs. The Pinot Noir is also consistently fine. Freemark Abbey Winery's production capacity is 24,000 cases per year. The wines are sold in 40 states.

ABOVE *This apparatus automatically monitors the sulfur dioxide level in the fermenting must and is here being checked by Freemark Abbey's winemaker, Larry Langbehn. The yeast sediment has to be drawn out of these polyurethane foam insulated tanks* (BELOW).

E & J Gallo Winery

Born within 100 miles of Modesto, Ernest and Julio Gallo grew up working in a small vineyard owned by their father, an immigrant from Italy's Piedmont region. Shortly after Repeal, the brothers began to make their own wine. They were successful almost immediately. In 1942, Ernest and Julio acquired the American Vineyard in Livingston, south of Modesto. The vineyard, covering over 1,000 acres, was planted to over 400 experimental wine varieties, beginning a long Gallo history of research in winemaking. Today, Gallo is the world's largest producer of premium quality wines.

Outstanding table wines from Gallo include Red Rosé, Hearty Burgundy and Chablis Blanc. Reserve Chablis and Reserve Burgundy are also made; these represent very good value. Among the varietals, French Colombard, Chenin Blanc, Gewürztraminer and Johannisberg Riesling are very good. Limited Release Cabernet Sauvignon and Limited Release Chardonnay are excellent.

RIGHT *The Gallo Winery is situated in the Dry Creek Valley of Sonoma County. The soil here is suitable for growing a wide range of varietals.*

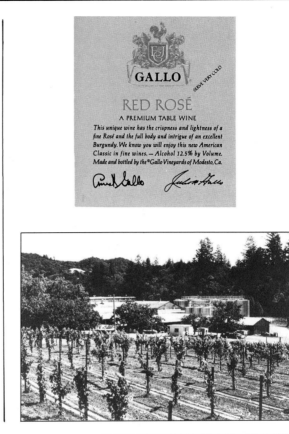

Glen Ellen Winery

The ranch where four generations of the Benzinger family now live has been in existence since 1868. In 1870, it produced some 30,000 gallons of brandy, but Prohibition sent it into oblivion. The property was rescued in 1979 by the Benzingers, who planted 40 acres of grapes (25 of them in Cabernet) in the southern end of the Sonoma Valley, in the Carneros district. The first crush at Glen Ellen was in 1981 — 3,000 cases were produced. The maximum production level is set at 25,000 cases a year.

For such a new operation, Glen Ellen already produces some impressive wines, which have won several awards. Chardonnay from Glen Ellen is a fruity, subtle and crisp wine; the Sauvignon Blanc has a grassy, flinty character with a clean finish. The Cabernet Sauvignon is a medium-bodied wine with a clean, varietal character. Proprietor's Reserve Red and Proprietor's Reserve White are excellent table wines and they are also very reasonably priced.

Grand Cru Vineyards

Since its founding in 1970, Grand Cru Vineyards in the Sonoma Valley has been dedicated to producing a limited selection of vintage varietals. In 1981, Bettina and Walter Dreyer became Grand Cru's sole owners. In that same year they doubled production capacity to 50,000 cases annually, although this still places the winery well within the small range by industry standards.

Co-founder and winemaker Bob Magnani continues to produce wines with a distinct style. The dry 1981 Chenin Blanc, produced from Sacramento River Delta grapes, has a crisp and delicate texture with low alcohol. The 1981 Sauvignon Blanc has complex, rich flavors and finesse, without the usual grassy-herbaceous character of this varietal. Two Cabernets, both intense with rich colors, are currently available: the 1979 Alexander Valley and the 1980 Northern California. Grand Cru Vineyards is perhaps best known for its outstanding, award-winning Gewürztraminers. The 1981 Alexander Valley is slightly sweet, with rich fruit and a spicy character.

GRGICH HILLS CELLARS

Mike Grgich (pronouced Gur-gich) is the winemaster who made Chateau Montelena's famous 1973 Chardonnay. That wine, which won a prestigious blind tasting in Paris over French wines, did a great deal to change the world's view of California vintages.

In 1977, Grgich joined with Austin E. Hills of the Hills Brothers coffee family to create Grgich Hills Cellar in the heart of the Napa Valley. Superb Chardonnay continues to be the main attraction, accounting for half the winery's annual production of 10,000 cases.

The 1980 Grgich Hills Chardonnay won top honors at the Los Angeles Wine Festival. Superbly balanced, this dry young wine has the depth and breadth to become even finer with proper bottle aging. A new release from Grgich Hills is the 1981 Fumé Blanc, a dry, elegantly soft and delicate wine. The 1981 early harvest Johannisberg Riesling is crisp and aromatic; the 1980 late harvest Riesling is subtly luscious, and made from naturally botrytized fruit. Alexander Valley Zinfandel, which is made from the fruit of 70-year-old hillside vines, is totally dry, and has an exceptional depth and complexity to it.

GUENOC WINERY

Guenoc Valley, part of the historic 23,000-acre Guenoc Ranch spanning the Lake and Napa County line, was once the home of the famed British beauty and actress Lillie Langtry. Her house and the stable are still standing on the grounds of Guenoc Winery, and owners Orville and Bob Magoon have restored Langtry House with Victorian antiques. Old records show that in 1891 Langtry Farms produced 50 tons of "Burgundy wine." Nowadays, the 270-acre vineyard is planted mostly in Bordeaux varietals (Cabernet Sauvignon, Merlot, Malbec, Petite Verdot, Cabernet Franc), with some Zinfandel and Petite Sirah. Whites include Chardonnay, Chenin Blanc, Sauvignon Blanc and Semillon. The winery is equipped to handle a projected production of 100,000 cases a year.

Guenoc's first wines were released in 1982 to much acclaim. Well-received so far have been the 1981 Chenin Blanc, the 1980 Cabernet Sauvignon and the 1981 Zinfandel. As more wines are released, this will be a vineyard to remember.

GUNDLACH-BUNDSCHU WINE COMPANY

After Paul Masson Vineyards, Gundlach-Bundschu Wine Company is probably the oldest vineyard in Calfornia still in the hands of the original family. Jacob Gundlach reached San Francisco in 1851 by way of a harrowing voyage (including being shipwrecked around Cape Horn). He quickly established the Rhinefarm Vineyards in the Sonoma Valley and prospered as a vintner. In 1876, Charles Bundschu joined the venture and married Gundlach's daughter. The firm survived devastating attacks of phylloxera and the 1906 earthquake and fire, but Prohibition meant the end of the winery. The vineyards survived, however, and in 1969 the great-great-grandchildren of both partners began reviving the historic winery. The first modern vintage was in 1973 and about 40,000 cases of high-quality, award-winning varietals are now produced each year at the vineyards.

All Gundlach-Bundschu wines are made from the fruit of fully mature vines, giving the wines extremely good varietal flavor. Among the most interesting are the 1979 Merlot, with a complex flavor and long, lingering finish and the 1981 Sonoma Riesling, with intense fruitiness and bouquet. The 1979 Zinfandel took a gold medal at the 1981 Sonoma County Fair.

HACIENDA WINE CELLARS

Within Buena Vista Vineyards, on the road to Hacienda Wine Cellars, a sign commemorates Count Agoston Haraszthy. In 1862, this Hungarian nobleman planted in these vineyards the first fine European grapes grown extensively in America. The resulting vineyards attracted dedicated wine-growers throughout California, with whom he freely shared cuttings. Haraszthy is acknowledged as the father of California viticulture; these vineyards are now a landmark.

The beautiful Buena Vista Vineyards are now owned by Frank H. Bartholomew, an international journalist. He purchased the property in 1941, restored it to production by 1949, and in 1973 established Hacienda Wine Cellars. Grapes are supplied by the Buena Vista Vineyard and Oat Valley Farm at Cloverdale and by selected vineyards from the Sonoma County area. Annual production is 18,000 cases.

The Chardonnay is barrel-fermented, while the other white and red wines are fermented in temperature-controlled stainless steel tanks. The Chardonnay is then aged in oak barrels, as are the reds: Cabernet Sauvignon, Zinfandel and Pinot Noir. The other white wines — Gewürztraminer, Johannisberg Riesling and Chenin Blanc — are made to preserve varietal flavor in the bottle.

HANZELL VINEYARDS

In the history of California wines, Hanzell Vineyards plays an important part. The winery was founded by Ambassador James D. Zellerbach in 1957, with the intent of reproducing the wines of Burgundy. To that end, he imported French wine-making equipment and planted French Pinot Chardonnay and Pinot Noir root cuttings on 35 acres in the hills of Sonoma County. Zellerbach was successful. His wines were soon so good that they were indistinguishable from French versions — an important moment for American wine-makers. Sadly, Zellerbach died suddenly in 1963. The property was sold and its wines declined, but in 1976 a new owner installed Robert Sessions as winemaker. The quality has been climbing steadily upward again, though production is still quite limited — around 3,000 cases a year.

The estate-bottled Pinot Noir is made in the Burgundian style and is rich and full-bodied. The 1978 release is a good example. The Chardonnay, also estate-bottled, is a prototype of the variety. In the Burgundian style, it is fruity and elegant, with a subtle touch of oak. The 1980 vintage is very fine.

HEITZ WINE CELLARS

A family-owned winery making fine wines in the Napa Valley since 1961, Heitz Wine Cellars products have acquired national acclaim. Cabernet Sauvignon and Chardonnay are the two wines with which Heitz Cellars has achieved much of its reputation for greatness.

The Heitz family owns vineyard acreage in the Napa Valley. The largest property is given over to the specialty grapes Grignolino and to Zinfandel.

BELOW *The Heitz Wine Cellars uses these huge white oak barrels for settling and clarification of both their red and white wines. These containers have a capacity for 1,000 to 2,000 gallons. The length of time each wine spends in the barrels varies. Cabernet Sauvignon, for example, will spend about 1½ years in them, whereas a Riesling or Gewürztraminer only six months.*

They also own two blocks of Chardonnay grapes. Cabernet Sauvignon grapes are bought, chiefly from the much-praised Martha's Vineyard in the western foothills of the Napa Valley. Other fine Cabernets come from selected quality vineyards. The Heitz Cellars Martha's Vineyard Cabernet Sauvignon is the standard by which other California Cabernets are judged.

It is not uncommon for 10 Cabernets to appear on the Heitz Cellars list when a new vintage is

1977
CALIFORNIA
GEWURZ TRAMINER
ALCOHOL 23% BY VOLUME
BOTTLED IN OUR CELLAR BY
HEITZ WINE CELLARS
ST. HELENA, CALIFORNIA

released in February. Chardonnay may also make multiple appearances on the list. Those labeled "Z" come from a family vineyard; others come from a blend of vineyards. The specialty Grignolino Rosé makes an annual appearance, though a short-lived one due to strong demand for this flavorful and bone-dry summer refresher. The Heitz list also includes Johannisberg Riesling, Chablis, Barbera, Grignolino, Burgundy, and Brut and Extra Dry Champagne-style wine every year. From time to time the Heitz label offers Gewürztraminer and Pinot Noir, but only when excellent grapes can be found for them.

HOFFMAN MOUNTAIN RANCH

The Paso Robles area of California, in the Santa Lucia Mountains, has been compared with the great Burgundy region of France, with its chalk and limestone soil. The Hoffman family, headed by Dr. Stanley Hoffman, a noted cardiologist, was the first to plant top varietal grapes in San Luís Obispo County in 1965. They marketed their first wine in 1972 and built their large winery in 1975. Their wines, especially their Pinot Noirs, have been winning awards ever since.

In 1982 the Hoffman Mountain Ranch underwent a financial reorganization, but the family still retains a substantial partnership. Production continues to rise, with 30,000 cases projected for 1983. In addition to their famous Pinot Noirs, the Hoffmans produce fine Cabernet Sauvignon and Zinfandel. Their delicate, fruity Chardonnay has won several gold medals, and they also produce excellent Johannisberg Riesling, Franken Riesling and Chenin Blanc.

HOP KILN WINERY AT GRIFFIN VINEYARD

The old stone and wood hop kiln at Griffin Vineyard is a registered California historical landmark. Marty Griffin restored the 80-year-old structure in 1975 and began making wine from his own vineyard there in the same year. Since then, Hop Kiln Winery wines have won more than 40 major awards. Most have come for the winery's vintage-dated varietals, but an Italian-styled red table wine called Marty Griffin's Big Red and a white Colombard-Riesling blend called "A Thousand Flowers" have also won awards. Production is well under 10,000 cases a year.

Among Hop Kiln's 11 wines are three superb varietals. The 1980 Zinfandel is rich and minty and the 1978 Zinfandel was judged to be the best wine from any Sonoma County winery at the 1980 Sonoma County Harvest Fair. Gewürztraminer is another Hop Kiln classic. It is bone dry, full-bodied and delicate. The Petite Sirah is made in the peppery, Rhône style from pre-Prohibition vines. Hop Kiln has just released a new, handmade sparkling white wine called Verveux. It is not distributed for sale, but is only available on the winery premises itself.

HUSCH VINEYARDS

One of the older Mendocino County wineries, Husch Vineyards is a small, family operation. It is situated in the Anderson Valley at the western end of the county, where the cool climate is ideal for growing Pinot Noir, Gewürztraminer and Chardonnay grapes. The H.A. Oswald family, which owns and operates the winery, has been raising grapes for over 20 years in the warmer Ukiah Valley of the county. From their home vineyard there, La Ribera, come the Sauvignon Blanc and Cabernet Sauvignon. All five Husch wines are estate-bottled; annual production is around 5,000 cases.

All recent Husch releases have been award-winning successes. The 1981 Chardonnay took a gold medal at the 1982 Los Angeles County Fair. Rich and full-bodied, it was aged for six months in Limousin oak. The 1981 Sauvignon Blanc, harvested from the home vineyard, has characteristic grassiness complemented by rich fruity flavors. Another gold-medal winner is the 1981 Gewürztraminer, with good sugar/acid balance and typical spiciness.

The chateau at Inglenook Vineyards (TOP) *was built nearly a century ago, by the founder of the vineyards, Captain Gustave Niebaum. John Richburg, winemaker, is in the wine library there* (ABOVE).

INGLENOOK VINEYARDS

Inglenook takes its name from the wooded "nooks" of the foothills of the Napa Valley. A Finnish sea captain named Gustave Niebaum came to the area in 1879 and began producing fine wines using cuttings from European chateaus. By the time of his death in 1908 Inglenook wines had at-

Joe Heitz (TOP), owner of Heitz Cellars, began winemaking on eight acres near St. Helena in the Napa Valley in 1961. Since then, he has built up a worldwide reputation for superb Cabernet Sauvignon and Chardonnay, as well as other fine wines. Only the finest grapes are used at Heitz Cellars; unripe or rotten grapes are carefully removed by hand before crushing begins (ABOVE). The rugged terrain of the Napa Valley reveals its volcanic origins. An aerial view (RIGHT) shows that most vines are planted on the valley floor, although some are grown on its wooded hillsides. Heitz's grapes come from its own vineyards and from those of contract growers in the valley.

ABOVE *The winery at Iron Horse Vineyards was built in 1979. Grapes from their properties in western Sonoma County and the Alexander Valley are vinified here.*

tained an international reputation. The winery was later run by Niebaum's great-nephew, John Daniel, Jr. As he approached retirement in 1964, Daniel sold the winery to United Vintners. It was sold again in 1969 and then purchased by the Heublein Corporation. The vineyards have been in continuous production over the years.

Inglenook table wines are grouped under three labels: Navalle, Vintage and Estate Bottled. The Estate Bottled varietal wines are made from grapes grown in the Napa Valley and include Chardonnay, Fumé Blanc, Grey Riesling, Chenin Blanc, Johannisberg Riesling, Gewürztraminer, Muscat Blanc, Gamay Rosé, Gamay Beaujolais, Pinot Noir, Zinfandel, Cabernet Sauvignon, Petite Sirah, and Charbono. A small amount of very high-quality wine is released each year under the designation Limited Cask.

IRON HORSE VINEYARDS

After a 15-year, worldwide search for a vineyard estate, Barry and Audrey Sterling purchased the Iron Horse Ranch in 1976. In partnership with Forrest Tancer, their first wine, an Alexander Valley Cabernet Sauvignon, was produced in 1978. In 1979, the winery was built and Iron Horse Vineyards crushed its first 6,000 cases of Chardonnay, Pinot Noir and Cabernet Sauvignon.

The wines of Iron Horse Vineyards are entirely grown, produced and bottled on the estate. On the ranch itself in western Sonoma County 55 acres of Chardonnay and 55 acres of Pinot Noir are grown. Tancer grows Zinfandel, Cabernet Sauvignon and Sauvignon Blanc on his Alexander Valley ranch, where the climate is warmer. A significant amount of effort goes into producing high-quality sparkling wines at Iron Horse. The champagne-style wines just released include a Brut that is a blend of Pinot Noir and Chardonnay, a Blanc de Blancs that is entirely Chardonnay, and a Blanc de Noirs that is entirely Pinot Noir.

Total production at Iron Horse is 20,000 cases a year. Two notable recent releases are the 1980 Pinot Noir, with a clean finish to a rich, intense flavor and the 1981 Chardonnay, with an austere, almost flinty style.

JEKEL VINEYARD

The extraordinarily long, cool growing season in the Arroyo Seco district of Monterey County was the primary reason Gus and Bill Jekel chose it for the site of their new vineyards in 1972. At the time they planted 140 acres of premium varietal grapes as the first step toward a family-owned wine estate. The winery was built in 1978 and expanded to a capactiy of 35,000 cases a year in 1981.

The style derives from the unique growing season, which results in wines of intense fruit and a fine balance of acids and tannins. The Johannisberg Riesling from Jekel is of consistently high quality, as is the Pinot Blanc. The Chardonnays are aged in French oak barrels to achieve a rich, complex finish. The cool climate and rocky soil of the vineyards are ideal to produce a superior Pinot Noir; with its excellent Cabernet Sauvignon, Jekel has attracted international attention.

JOHNSON'S ALEXANDER VALLEY WINERY

The small Johnson winery, with an annual production of only 10,000 cases, is a family endeavor by the Johnson brothers Jay, Tom and Will. They produce varietal wines, vintage-dated and estate-bottled, using grapes grown on their 70-acre vineyard along the Russian River in Sonoma County. The Johnsons began making wine in 1975, and they won five awards on their first three releases. They have since carried away many others, including a gold medal at the 1981 Orange County Fair for the winery's 1979 Johannisberg Riesling.

Among the varietals produced at the Johnson winery are a very good Pinot Noir and Chenin Blanc. Other wines include Cabernet Sauvignon, Gewürztraminer and Chardonnay. A sideline is the only pear wine produced in Sonoma County.

KALIN CELLARS

Kalin Cellars is a small winery located in Marin County on San Francisco Bay. It produces 5,000 cases a year of wine made by completely traditional European methods. These time- and labor-intensive procedures severely limit the quantity — but not the quality — of wine produced. Distribution is very limited, as connoisseurs in San Francisco quickly buy up almost all that is available.

Kalin Cellars' red wines, including Cabernet Sauvignon, Pinot Noir and Zinfandel, are fermented for several weeks in wood *cuvées* and aged in new French oak barrels. These wines are neither fined nor filtered; rather, they are naturally clarified and stablized by settling and aging in the barrel. White wines, including Johannisberg Riesling, Semillon and Chardonnay, are both fermented and aged in new French oak barrels. These wines receive the minimum amount of fining necessary to achieve brilliance and stability and they are usually bottled without filtration.

Vineyard sources are selected for their superior soil type and situation in the coolest possible microclimate suitable for the variety grown. Kalin Cellars produces exclusively single-vineyard wines. The region of the vineyard, but not the name, is on the label.

ROBERT KEENAN WINERY

High up on the east side of Spring Mountain in the Napa Valley, the Robert Keenan Winery produces 7,000 cases a year of only two wines: Chardonnay and Cabernet Sauvignon. The 45 acres of vineyard at the winery produce about 85 percent of Keenan's needs. The first release of Chardonnay was in the spring of 1978, when the 1977 vin-

OVERLEAF *Grapes must be picked when their sugar content is exactly right. A refractometer is used to measure sweetness.*

tage was highly rated. Subsequent releases have also been excellent. The 1979 Napa Chardonnay, for example, has a gentle fruity flavor with a good balance of body and acid.

In 1979 Keenan Winery first released its 1977 Napa Valley Cabernet Sauvignon. This set a high standard that has since been consistently met or bettered. The 1978 vintage was sold out almost immediately and all 3,000 cases of later releases have also been bought up straightaway.

THE KONOCTI WINERY

California's smallest cooperative winery, the Konocti Winery, is in the heart of Lake County, a premium wine region. The winery was built in 1979 by a group of growers who were selling their grapes to some of the finest wineries in the state and then decided to make their own. Today, there are 26 participating vineyards in Konocti Winery. Most are family-owned and operated. In 1981, Konocti won 11 awards at major Calfornia wine competitions. The annual production is 35,000 cases of excellent varietals at reasonable prices.

One of the best buys in wine now available is the 1979 Konocti Cabernet Sauvignon. Medium garnet in color, it has an aroma suggestive of chocolate and violets. Another great bargain is the 1980 Late Harvest Johannisberg Riesling, with high residual sugar balanced by the acid content to make an eminently drinkable wine.

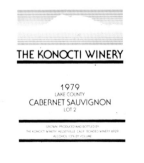

HANNS KORNELL CHAMPAGNE CELLARS

A third-generation Champagne master, Hanns Kornell fled the Nazis and arrived penniless in America in 1940. By 1952 he had saved enough to make a small beginning with his own sparkling white wine in a rented winery in Sonoma. Six years later he found his current location, the historic stone Larkmead Cellars just north of St. Helena in the heart of the Napa Valley. He now makes over 100,000 cases a year of award-winning sparkling wine, using the traditional *méthode champenoise*, including hand riddling and candle inspection of the bottles.

The German style is evident in Kornell's driest variety, made primarily from Riesling grapes and labeled "Sehr Trocken," German for "very dry." This superior wine is now available in a vintage-dated release. Brut Champagne from Kornell is also made with Riesling grapes. This very dry wine has won a number of gold medals at international tastings. A slightly softer sparkling wine, Kornell Extra Dry is made with a mixture of Semillon, Sauvignon Blanc and Chenin Blanc grapes. Kornell Rosé Champagne is unusually dry yet full of flavor; the Rouge is a full-bodied red sparkling wine. Kornell also makes an interesting Muscat Alexandria, an excellent champagne-style dessert wine.

ABOVE *The historic stone aging vaults of Hanns Kornell Champagne Cellars are listed in the National Register of Historic Places. The cellars were built in 1906.*

CHARLES KRUG WINERY

A pioneer winemaker in the Napa Valley, Charles Krug founded his winery in 1861. His wines were proclaimed outstanding by the gourmets of his day, both at home and abroad and his reputation grew. But in the 1880s, phylloxera killed off many of his vines and the Krug reputation faded. In 1943, Cesare Mondavi, patriarch of the Mondavi wine family, bought the company and built a highly successful business in California jug wines. The winery is still under the personal supervision of members of the Mondavi family. It sells millions of half-gallon jugs each year, but also produces a full range of premium varietal wines under the Charles Krug label. The winery uses grapes from the vineyards of the Napa Valley.

Choice lots of Charles Krug Cabernet Sauvignon are labeled as Cesare Mondavi Vintage Selections. The 1977 release, now available, is lush and full-bodied, with a rich, dark color. Among the white wines, the Chenin Blanc, a new variety from Krug, is medium-dry with a fruity bouquet. The Chardonnay is medium-bodied and dry, with characteristic varietal flavor.

LONG VINEYARDS

A tiny operation producing fewer than 2,000 cases a year, Long Vineyards is owned and run by Bob and Zelma Long. Zelma is winemaker at Simi Winery; Bob handles day-to-day operations. The 15 acres of vineyard were established in 1967 and the winery built 10 years later. Despite distribution that is limited to a mailing list and a few retail outlets, Long Vineyards wines have an enthusiastic following.

Rich, fruity Chardonnay is entirely barrel-fermented in French oak and then aged for two years in barrels and bottles. The superb Riesling is made in the late harvest style, with an alcohol level of 10 percent and residual sugar levels of five to 10 percent, depending on the year. The Longs have just begun to produce a third wine, Cabernet Sauvignon (as yet unreleased) from grapes grown in Yountville by the University of California, Davis. They hope the wine will show the value of the University's research efforts.

LYTTON SPRINGS WINERY

Producing only Zinfandel, Lytton Springs Winery is located between the Alexander and Dry Creek Valleys in Sonoma County. The winery is situated on the property of one of the eldest and finest Zinfandel vineyards in the state, Valley Vista Vineyards, owned by Richard Sherwin. Many of the vines were planted by Italian immigrants at the turn of the century. The first vintage at Lytton Springs was that of 1975. Production now is around 10,000 cases a year, divided between Valley Vista Vineyard and Sonoma County Zinfandels. The wine is not filtered, but it is racked several times during the aging process.

MARKHAM WINERY

Before there was a Markham Winery, there were Markham vineyards on 285 prime Napa Valley acres in three locations. Since 1975, premium wineries have been selecting these vineyards to supply them with their grapes. Winemaking began at Markham in 1978; all wines under the Markham label are estate-bottled, with a vineyard designation on the label. About 25,000 cases of vintage-dated varietals are produced each year.

The imposing facade of the old winery at Paul Masson (FAR LEFT) comes from a church in San Jose that was badly damaged by the great earthquake in 1906. The winery is now one of the largest in the United States. The Paul Masson vineyards are in Monterey County, near Soledad, Greenfield and King City. White grapes (BELOW) are brought from the scattered vineyards in two-ton gondolas, which are carried on a flatbed truck. To keep the grapes from oxidizing in transit, they may be given a dusting of sulfur dioxide before leaving the vineyard. This has no effect on the flavor of the wine. Dissolved oxygen in bottled wines, however, can harm their flavor. To prevent this, a vacuum is created in the headspace above the wine before the cork is inserted at the modern Masson sterile bottling line (LEFT).

The 1979 Markham Muscat de Frontignan is a sweet, medium-bodied wine, with an elegantly powerful aroma. It is an excellent aperitif or light dessert wine. Cabernet Sauvignon from Markham's Yountville vineyard is known for its aromatic complexity; 1978 was an especially good year. French oak is used to age the dry Chenin Blanc and the Chardonnay, giving both full-bodied flavors. Johannisberg Riesling from Markham is a slighly sweet wine with pronounced varietal aromas. An intense, smooth Merlot is sold under the Vin Mark label.

The core of the Markham winery (BELOW) *was built in 1876. The Markhams and their general manager are inspecting a Cabernet Sauvignon vine* (RIGHT).

MARK WEST VINEYARDS

In the Russian River area of the Sonoma Valley, south of Healdsburg, the days are sunny and the nights cool and foggy. Mark West Vineyards is located on 116 rolling acres near the river in this ideal microclimate. Joan and Bob Ellis established the winery in 1976, naming it after the frost-preventing creek that is on the property. The creek itself took its name from Marcus West, an early pioneer. The 60 acres of vineyards were planted with Chardonnay, Johannisberg Riesling, Gewürztraminer and Pinot Noir grapes in 1974; plans are to expand the plantings to 80 acres in the near future. Current production is 11,000 cases annually, with the projected production targeted at 25,000 cases of estate-bottled wines.

The Mark West 1980 Chardonnay, made with grapes from the Wasson Ranch in Alexander Valley, has attracted favorable notice, as has the estate-bottled 1979 Chardonnay and 1979 Pinot Noir. The 1980 and 1981 Gewürztraminers are also excellent. A new aperitif wine called Pinot Angelica has been created by winemaker Joan Ellis. Lush and fruity, with natural sweetness balanced by the high acidity of early harvested Pinot Noir grapes, Pinot Angelica is fresh and light with a romantic style.

LOUIS M. MARTINI WINERY

Louis Michael Martini arrived in San Francisco in 1900, a 12-year-old immigrant from Italy. He began making wine with his father and by 1922 Louis M. Martini Grape Products Co. was established. The company weathered Prohibition by producing altar wine. By 1933 the present winery in St. Helena was built and in 1936 the Monte Rosso vineyard in the Sonoma Valley was purchased. Today, Martini Winery remains a family-owned and family-run corporation. The five vineyards in Napa and Sonoma Counties cover some 800 acres planted to premium varietal grapes, with a joint annual production of about 325,000 cases.

Martini wines are known for their informative labels and excellent value. As quality merits, limited amounts of Private Reserve and Special Selection wines are produced. Noteworthy under these labels are the Cabernet Sauvignons. Martini is probably the only winemaker in America to produce varietal Folle Blanche. This relatively rare grape is sometimes used in anonymous jug wines. Among dessert wines, Martini Moscato Amabile is widely known and much loved.

1981

FOLLE BLANCHE

PRODUCED AND BOTTLED AT THE WINERY BY

LOUIS M. MARTINI

ST. HELENA, NAPA COUNTY, CALIFORNIA, U.S.A.
12% ALCOHOL BY VOLUME

PAUL MASSON VINEYARDS

Paul Masson Vineyards was founded in 1852 and is the oldest continuous wine-producer in California. Paul Masson emigrated from his native Burgundy to California when he was 19 in 1878. The vineyards he inherited and improved, along with his own plantings at the "Vineyard in the Sky" in the Santa Cruz Mountains, have grown until they now encompass 4,500 acres and four major production and aging facilities. These are the Pinnacles Vineyards in Monterey County, also the site of the Pinnacles Vineyard Winery; the Sherry Cellars in Madera; the Champagne and Wine Cellars in Saratoga; and the Wine Aging Cellars in San Jose. Paul Masson Vineyards produces a full line of 47 types of table wines, sparkling wines, ports, sherries, Madeira, vermouth and brandy. Sales of 7,000,000 cases a year rank Paul Masson fifth among all U.S. wineries.

There are too many Paul Masson products to be covered in detail, but the estate-bottled varietals from the Pinnacles Vineyards are of most interest to lovers of fine wines. Paul Masson has offered vintage-dated wines carrying the Monterey County appellation since 1977. The 1980 Fumé Blanc is a big, complex wine, aged in oak and with a distinct varietal flavor. Chardonnay from 1980 also has great varietal depth. This wine is aged in oak and is well-balanced, rich and textured, with a unique flinty taste. Dry and characteristically spicy, the 1981 Gewürztraminer is pleasantly aromatic. Other vintage-dated wines include Pinot Chardonnay, Johannisberg Riesling, Sauvignon Blanc, Cabernet Sauvignon, Pinot Noir and Gamay Beaujolais.

BELOW *Paul Masson winery was established in 1852 by Etienne Thée. He was succeeded by his son-in-law, Charles LeFranc, who was in turn succeeded by Paul Masson, his son-in-law. Masson died in 1940.*

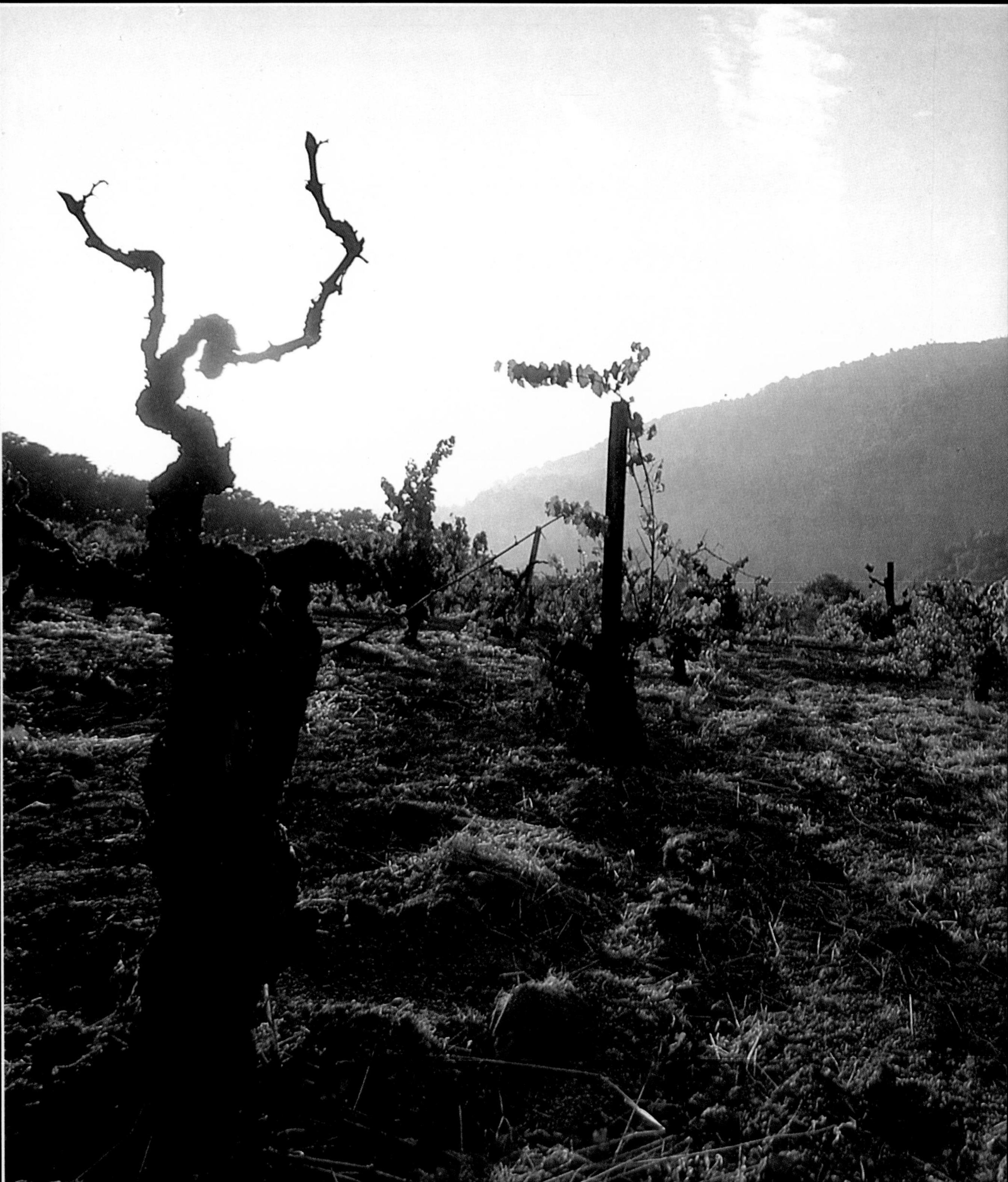

LEFT *The sun is rising over part of the massive 4,500 acres of Paul Masson Vineyards in Monterey County. There is such a variety of microclimates and soil structures within the vineyards that a huge number of different wines are produced. The vineyards were founded in 1852, so have had long experience in growing top quality grapes* (BELOW). *The pruning of the vines is as vital a stage in the cycle of the vine's culture, as the harvesting* (BOTTOM). *It controls the number and thus the quality of the grapes.*

MASTANTUONO WINERY

When the small, family-owned Mastantuono Winery began operations in 1977, it was one of five in the Paso Robles area of San Luis Obispo County. There are now some 15 wineries in the area but Mastantuono still stands out for its notable Zinfandels. Every vintage has won either a gold or silver medal, sometimes both, at important competitions. Including small lots of Cabernet Sauvignon, Chardonnay, Sauvignon Blanc and Muscat Canelli, annual production is 3,000 cases a year, although the new, recently opened winery will increase the output considerably. Mastantuono now has 15 acres of Zinfandel under cultivation and releases limited amounts of estate-bottled wine. Other grapes are purchased in the district, which is famous for its Zinfandel vineyards.

Mastantuono Zinfandels are natural wines, unfined and unfiltered. Their color is rich and dark; their flavor is intensely fruity, tannic and quite spicy. The label indicates the vineyard and vintage year. Regardless of year, the Zinfandels from Dusi Vineyard grapes are splendid.

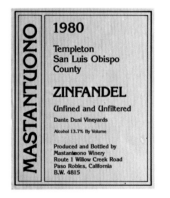

MATANZAS CREEK WINERY

Nestled beneath Bennett Peak in the Bennett Valley just south of Santa Rosa, the Matanzas Creek Winery is in an interesting position. While it is part of the Russian River watershed, its microclimate is more distinctly that of the Sonoma Valley, and the vineyard is considered part of the recently designated Sonoma Valley appellation. The first crush at Matanzas Creek took place in 1978, using grapes from various North Coast counties. Now, however, the winery uses only Sonoma County grapes.

Matanzas Creek wines include an estate-bottled Chardonnay, as well as Pinot Noir, Cabernet Sauvignon and Merlot. All show strong varietal character, with very good balance of fruit mixed with oak.

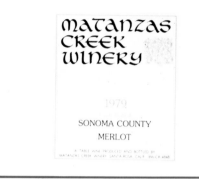

MAYACAMAS VINEYARDS

The Mayacamas Winery was originally built in 1889, but fell into disuse at the beginning of this century. The ancient, declining vineyards were replanted with Chardonnay and Cabernet Sauvignon vines in 1941 by Jack and Mary Taylor and sold in 1968 to the current owners, Robert and Elinor Travers. Now specializing in the wines of Mayacamas-grown grapes, Chardonnay and Cabernet Sauvignon, Mayacamas Vineyards produces about 2,000 cases a year of each. Some 600 to 800 cases a year each of Sauvignon Blanc and Pinot Noir or Zinfandel (not both in the same year) are also produced. The Travers produce their Cabernets and Chardonnays primarily from their own mountain-grown grapes, supplemented by other hillside purchases. The low tonnage produced by this type of vineyard yields intense fruit. The resultant wines require considerably longer than average to mature.

The mountain-grown grapes of Mayacamas Vineyards (ABOVE) *yield low tonnage but very intense fruit. The resulting wines require longer than average to mature.*

McDowell Valley Vineyards

Nestled in the southeast corner of Mendocino County, McDowell Valley has been identified by the federal government as a distinct viticultural area. The designation recognizes the valley's unique soils and microclimate and also its long wine-making history, which dates back to the 1890s. In 1970, Richard and Karen Keehn purchased 360 acres of prime vineyards in the heart of the valley. After developing the varietal quality of the vines, they built their modern winery in 1979, using sophisticated technology to create California's first solar winery.

McDowell Valley Vineyards produces estate-bottled wines exclusively from its own plantings, many of which are over 30 years old (some are nearly 70). These mature vines yield fruit with rich complex flavor. The Chenin Blanc is cold-fermented, achieving a delicate floral aroma and the Fumé Blanc and the Chardonnay both have a distinct varietal flavor. The McDowell Valley Grenache is a sophisticated rosé harvested from 30- to 60-year-old vines. Mature fruit from older vines is also used to produce Cabernet Sauvignon. Unfined and lightly filtered, this wine is big in structure, yet shows balance and finesse. Zinfandel from McDowell Valley is intense but well-balanced; Petite Sirah has strong character.

RIGHT *Reaping the grapes is helped by a harvesting sled. This contraption fits conveniently between the rows of vines and enables the picker to pile his baskets of grapes one on top of the other, without making endless journeys or knocking the vines. The time between flowering and harvest is reckoned to be about 100 days.*

BELOW LEFT *Comparative wine tasting sessions are a regular occurence among the staff at the Robert Mondavi Winery. It is a necessary procedure to test and improve the quality of each wine, and is also a method of training staff. Here,* (BELOW RIGHT) *a glass 'serpent' is being inserted into the top of a vat to prevent oxidation.* FAR RIGHT *The Robert Mondavi Winery is situated on his vineyards in the Napa Valley. Mondavi only opened this vineyard in 1966, but his storage capacity has already increased from 100,000 to nearly 2,000,000 gallons. It was the first entirely new winery to be constructed in the Napa Valley since the end of Prohibition and has remained one of the most progressive.*

MILANO VINEYARDS AND WINERY

Milano Winery is housed in one of Mendocino County's few remaining hop kilns. Jim Milone, a third-generation grape-grower, took over the hop kiln built by his father and grandfather in 1977. Since then, his wines have gained widespread recognition by winning many awards and tastings. The emphasis at Milano is on Chardonnay, accounting for nearly 80 percent of the 10,000 cases of wine made each year.

The 1981 Lolonis Vineyard Chardonnay is fruity and aromatic, it follows in the fine tradition of the 1981 release, which won a gold medal at the Orange County Fair. In addition to the Chardonnay, Milano also makes limited but increasing amounts of Cabernet Sauvignon. The grapes come from family vineyards in the Sanel Valley of Mendocino County. Milano produced a Late Harvest Riesling for the first time in 1981. This vintage was a two-time gold-medal winner; the 1982 vintage shows as much or more potential.

MILL CREEK VINEYARDS AND WINERY

The Kreck family, owners and operators of Mill Creek Vineyards, planted their first vines in 1965 in the Dry Creek Valley of Sonoma County. They later purchased a 65-acre vineyard on the site of a former prune orchard and began building their own winery. The first of their vintage-dated varietals was released in 1976. Since then, Mill Creek wines have received favorable comments and several awards.

Grapes for the Mill Creek Cabernet Sauvignon come from the family's vineyards near the winery and from their original Dry Creek plantings. It is their specialty wine and accounts for nearly half their annual production. The 1978 Chardonnay has a velvety texture with a lingering aftertaste; the grapes are field-crushed and the must allowed six hours of skin contact. Mill Creek is one of only a handful of wineries producing a varietal Merlot, which is similar to Cabernet Sauvignon, but with a softer finish. The Kreck family favorite is their Cabernet Blush, a rosé of Cabernet Sauvignon.

MIRASSOU VINEYARDS

Many California wine families can claim a long history in the business but only the Mirassous can claim five generations going back to 1854. The original Mirassou vineyards were in Santa Clara Valley until that rural area became increasingly populated. The family then began to plant vineyards in Monterey County, starting in 1961. Today, Mirassou Vineyards covers more than 1,000 acres. Until 1966, newly fermented Mirassou wines were sold in bulk to premium wineries for aging and sale under other labels. In that year the family decided to produce wines for national distribution under its own label. In 1966 1,000 cases were made; nearly 350,000 are now made each year.

All 18 of Mirassou's wines are vintage-dated and all are quite reasonably priced. Among the most interesting are the limited-production Harvest Selections, which receive extended aging, thus ensuring a fuller, more mature flavor. Also interesting is the L.D. (Late Disgorged) Champagne. All Mirassous champagne-types are made by the French *méthode champenoise*; the L.D. is distinguished by an assertive yeasty character developed by leaving the wine *en tirage* for at least four years.

ROBERT MONDAVI WINERY

Robert Mondavi's involvement in the California grape industry began when he was a child. He graduated from Stanford in 1936, and in 1948 he persuaded his family to buy the dormant Charles Krug Winery. Mondavi remained with Krug until 1965, when he founded his own winery. From the start, Mondavi has been an innovative leader in the wine world. For example, he was the first winemaker in the Napa Valley to put cold fermentation to optimum use and he has always been active in educating the public in the subtleties of fine wine. His vineyards now cover 1,000 acres; additional grapes are purchased by contract from independent growers. In 1980, Mondavi started a joint venture with Baron Phillipe de Rothschild of Chateau Mouton Rothschild to produce a limited quantity of premium Napa Valley wine. The first of these wines is scheduled for release early in 1984.

Of the many remarkable wines produced by Robert Mondavi Winery, Fumé Blanc and Chenin Blanc are particularly noteworthy. The Fumé Blanc is an unusual dry white wine made from Sauvignon Blanc grapes. Robert Mondavi was the first to popularize it. Chenin Blanc, until Mondavi began to produce it, was called White Pinot and was quite unpopular. Mondavi changed the name and the style; the wine is now well-regarded as moderately light, slightly sweet and fresh.

BELOW *The French oak aging casks at Mondavi Winery are used primarily for red wines, although sometimes for white. Barrel aging can last 4 to 10 months for whites.*

R. MONTALI WINERY

The Montali Winery combines the formidable talents of Ralph Montali, who has been connected with the wine industry for over 40 years and Dr. Richard Carey, formerly the owner of the Richard Carey Winery in San Leandro. Although this is a new operation, production in 1982 was already at 20,000 cases.

Premium wines that are produced and bottled by Richard Carey and R. Montali Winery include Zinfandel and Blanc Fumé from the Paso Robles region and Gamay Beaujolais, Cabernet Sauvignon, Chardonnay and Gewürztraminer from the Santa Maria Valley. Zinfandel from Amador County's Shenandoah Valley has recently been released. A special Blanc de Noir called La Belle Blanc is another new addition. Drier and fruity, this wine is a blend of White Cabernet, Zinfandel and Pinot Noir.

MONTEREY PENINSULA WINERY

The first crush at Monterey Peninsula Winery, in the autumn of 1974, produced a Cabernet Sauvignon that won a gold medal at the Los Angeles County Fair. The wine set the standard for this Monterey winery: wines that are 100 percent varietal, 100 percent from the vineyard of appellation, unfined and unfiltered and produced in very small lots. Monterey Peninsula often has as many as 10 to 15 separate lots of Zinfandel in a given year. The annual production of some 14,000 cases is made using grapes from the Salinas River drainage area, which includes Monterey, San Luis Obispo and Amador Counties.

Monterey Peninsula is known particularly for its red wines, especially Pinot Noir, Petite Sirah, Barbera, Cabernet Sauvignon and Zinfandel. The winery also makes an interesting, 100 percent varietal White Zinfandel and excellent Chardonnays and Pinot Blancs. When weather conditions are right, Monterey Peninsula produces late harvest wines. The 1979 Late Harvest Johannisberg Riesling is a notable example.

THE MONTEREY VINEYARD

Upper Monterey County has California's coolest grape-growing climate and longest growing season. The Monterey Vineyard is situated between Gabilan Heights and the Santa Lucia Mountains. The winery was built in 1974 and purchased by The Wine Spectrum, a subsidiary of the Coca-Cola Company of Atlanta, in 1977. Today, Monterey produces fine vintage-dated varietal wines, primarily of Monterey County appellation, three varietal-blend Classic California wines and Special Signature Selection wines of outstanding quality, such as Zinfandel, made from grapes harvested in December, and Nouveau Gamay Beaujolais, from what is believed to be the latest (or earliest) harvest ever to occur in the whole of the United States.

The Monterey Vineyard concentrates on producing excellent white varietal wines and a small percentage of red. The white wines include Gruner Sylvaner, a fruity wine made mainly from Sylvaner grapes, and they also produce a botrytized Sauvignon Blanc.

MONTEVINA WINES

The largest foothill winery in California, Montevina Wines is located in the Shenandoah Valley of Amador County, in the foothills of the High Sierras. The 450 acres of vineyards are planted to Zinfandel, Sauvignon Blanc, Cabernet and Barbera at an elevation of 1,700 feet. Wine production began in 1973 and current volume is now 40,000 cases a year.

Montevina wines are known for their intense varietal flavors. This is particularly true of the Zinfandels, which are big, bold wines suitable for long aging in the bottle. Sauvignon Blanc from Montevina is also very intense and fruity; Cabernet Sauvignon is the same, but strongly tannic.and ideally suited to long aging.

J.W. MORRIS WINERIES

The founders of J.W. Morris originally planned to produce only port wine. That plan has changed somewhat since 1975 and they now produce red and white varietal wines as well. The wines are made chiefly from grapes purchased in the Sonoma area, with the vineyards usually designated on the label. Port is now only about 20 percent of the annual production of 12,000 cases.

Three ports, Sonoma County Vintage Port from 1979, the undated Founders California Port and Amador County Angelica are fine examples of the J.W. Morris approach to this wine. Among the varietals, the 1981 California Select bottlings of Chardonnay, Zinfandel and Sauvignon Blanc stand out. Morris also makes generic table wines under the names White Private Reserve and Red Private Reserve.

MOUNT EDEN VINEYARDS

Mount Eden Vineyards has a long and somewhat tangled history. Originally owned by the famed but quarrelsome Martin Ray, control passed to a group of new owners, who made Dick Graff, of Chalone Vineyard, winemaker. The standard set by Martin Ray has been maintained, as has his policy of limited production and high prices. The 23-acre vineyard at Mount Eden is located near the peak of the mountain in Santa Clara, at an elevation of nearly 2,000 feet. All estate-bottled wines from Mount Eden come from this vineyard.

Mount Eden can be relied on to produce classic examples of Chardonnay. The 1979 release is toasty, with a spicy nose. The 1981 Ventana Vineyards Chardonnay, released under the subsidiary MEV label, is excellent value. Pinot Noirs from Mount Eden are also consistently superb. The vintages of 1972, 1974, 1975 and 1977, all estate-bottled, are outstanding. Also outstanding are the 1978 and 1979 Cabernet Sauvignons.

MOUNT VEEDER WINERY

With only 20 acres of vines on the steep slopes of Mount Veeder in the Napa Valley, this winery produces about 4,000 cases a year, most of it Cabernet Sauvignon. The owners, Michael and Arlene Bernstein, planted their first vines in 1965, but did not begin producing wine until 1973. In 1978 they reached their goal of producing wines made only from their own vineyards.

From 1973 through 1976 Mount Veeder Cabernet Sauvignon was made using only grapes from the Bernstein Vineyards. Beginning with the first harvests of Merlot, Malbec, Cabernet Franc and

MAIN PICTURE *At Joseph Phelps Vineyards, young vines are protected from frost and bad weather during the winter months. In summer, however, it is often too hot and dry so water pumps have been installed to improve irrigation* (ABOVE). *Grapes are always handpicked on this vineyard and carried in any available container* (INSET LEFT).

Petite Verdot in 1977, the Cabernets are now blended for added complexity and softness. They are rich, full and tannic, with vivid varietal character and excellent aging potential. Mount Veeder also produces full-flavored Zinfandels; recommended vintages are 1978 and 1980. The 1981 Chenin Blanc has a very distinctive character, aromatic with a full-bodied, long finish.

NAVARRO VINEYARDS

Navarro is a small, owner-operated winery in the Anderson Valley, a cool coastal area of Mendocino County very similar to Alsace in viticultural climate. Gewürztraminer, Chardonnay and Pinot Noir are estate-grown, with additional Chardonnay and Riesling grapes obtained from neighboring vineyards.

The cool ocean breezes and twice-daily fog of the Anderson Valley are ideal for Gewürztraminer and it is with this wine that Navarro Vineyards has made its mark. The 1981 Late Harvest is light gold with amber highlights; it is full-bodied with ripe botrytis aromas. Its natural sweetness is balanced by good acidity. The dry estate-bottled 1981 is full-bodied, with a spicy, lingering finish.

Navarro also produces a Gewürztraminer/White Riesling blend called Edelzwicker. The 1981 vintage is a pale straw-yellow in color, with low alcohol and a smooth, spicy finish. The Navarro 1980 estate-bottled Gewürztraminer has won several medals, including a silver at the 1982 Orange County Fair.

NOVITIATE WINERY

Two problems faced the early Jesuit Fathers and Brothers in 1888. How could they support the novices training to become Jesuits, and where could they obtain sacramental wine for serving Mass? The solution to both problems was found by Brother Louis Olivier. A vintner in his early days in southern France, he sent home to Montpellier for cuttings of its best varietal grapes. The tradition started by Brother Olivier has been handed down to this day. The current cellarmaster is Brother Lee Williams, who has been making wine at the Novitiate Winery for more than 25 years.

Novitiate produces a number of excellent wines at Los Gatos, in the green foothills of the Santa Cruz Mountains. Among the fine white dinner wines are Chateau Novitiate, a mildly sweet wine of the Sauterne type. Light gold in color, it features a rich bouquet and full taste. A light, delicate, and refreshing Johannisberg Riesling is also made, along with a dry Malvasia, made the white Muscat grapes. This unusual wine is slightly sweet, with just a hint of spice.

Novitiate makes four sherrys, including Flor, which is very dry, full-bodied and quite rare. An interesting dessert wine is Novitiate Black Muscat, made from the Muscat Hamburg grape; it has a unique, rich taste approaching that of a liqueur.

PARDUCCI WINE CELLARS

The founder of the Parducci Wine Cellars, Adolph Parducci, was a pioneer winemaker in Mendocino County, planting his first vines in 1931. The Parducci family has continued to produce fine varietal wines from their own grapes at a reasonable cost ever since.

Among the robust red wines are a full-bodied Cabernet Sauvignon, an earthy Petite Sirah, a velvety Pinot Noir and a fresh, fruity Zinfandel. The Parducci Gamay Beaujolais is their most popular wine. The Parducci style of winemaking is evident in their straightforward Chardonnay and estate-bottled Chenin Blanc. The addition of a small amount of Semillon gives their Sauvignon Blanc an added dimension, while their Medocino Riesling combines Sylvaner Riesling and French Colombard for a wine of lively tartness. The cool climate and high quality of Parducci's grapes create a perfectly balanced Gewürztraminer.

Occasionally, in some vineyards, small quantities of extremely fine wines are produced; they are aged in small oak cooperage and held for an extended period of time. At that point, if their quality is still judged to be superior, they are designated as Cellar Master Selections and the Parducci crest is affixed to the label.

BELOW *This is a stemmer from the Parducci Wine Cellars, which separates the grapes from their stems.*

J. PEDRONCELLI WINERY

Located near Geyserville in Sonoma County, the J. Pedroncelli Winery nestles among the rolling hills of a winding canyon near Dry Creek Valley. John Pedroncelli, Sr. purchased the property in 1927 because it reminded him of his native Lombardy. During Prohibition, Pedroncelli sold field-mixed grapes from his vineyards to home winemakers. After Repeal, the family began making wine, selling it in bulk to other wineries. As one of the first to switch from bulk wine processing to premium varietals, Pedroncelli Winery began selling Zinfandel in 1949.

More than 30 years later, John Jr. and his brother Jim produce 125,000 cases of fine varietal wines a year. The grapes come from their 135 acres of vineyards and from growers in the Dry Creek and Alexander Valleys. These vintage-dated varietals are reasonably priced.

Of the many wines made by J. Pedroncelli Winery, several are recommended above the others. The Johannisberg Riesling is slightly tart and fruity, with a touch of sweetness in the finish. Chardonnay is full-bodied, dry, and crisp; Gewürztraminer is delicate with a floral spiciness. Drier than most rosés, Zinfandel Rosé retains a fruity character without heavy tannins.

JOSEPH PHELPS VINEYARDS

The wines of Joseph Phelps Vineyards made their debut with the vintage of 1973. The winery and home vineyards are in Spring Valley, a small fold in the hills east of St. Helena. In planting just 220 of his 670 acres, owner Joseph Phelps preserved Spring Valley's peaceable nature, yet was able to adapt sites to grape varieties of a very high standard. But the home vineyards, diverse as they are, cannot satisfy every requirement for quantity and quality. Phelps therefore purchases grapes from selected ranches, identifying the finest on his wine labels. The Eisele and Backus vineyards are good examples.

All Phelps wines are remarkably good, but the Rieslings and Gewürztraminers stand out, perhaps because of winemaker Walter Schug's German background. The 1981 Johannisberg Riesling is delicate and fruity, with a slightly tart edge. The off-dry finish of the 1981 Gewürztraminer combines beautifully with its spicy, nutty flavor. An unusual Phelps wine is the 1980 Scheurebe Late Harvest. This wine, made from grapes that are a Riesling cross, is lively and fruity, with the barest trace of muscat. It is made in the German auslese style.

The Insignia program at Phelps Vineyards selects the best of the red wine vintage, and highlights its excellence through special aging, special labels and a special price. The 1978 Insignia combined Cabernet Sauvignon, Merlot and Cabernet Franc for a deep, powerful blend.

PIPER SONOMA

A new venture, Piper Sonoma combines 200 years of French Champagne history with the adventuresome spirit of California winemaking at its best. The company was formed in 1980 to combine the experience of the famed Champagne producer Piper Heidsieck of France with that of Rodney Strong of Sonoma Vineyards, one of

California's most highly respected winemakers. With the release of its first wines in 1982, Piper Sonoma made a promising start toward its goal of producing fine sparkling wines in the very best tradition of the *méthode champenoise*. Production at Piper Sonoma is limited. Only 28,000 cases of Piper Sonoma Brut, with 5,000 cases of Blanc de Noirs and 2,500 cases of Tête de Cuvée, were produced from the 1980 vintage.

The 1980 Brut was very successfully received. The recently released Blanc de Noirs is made entirely from Pinot Noir grapes from Sonoma Vineyards. It has a finely balanced varietal character and is a pale straw color without a trace of pink.

RIGHT *A Vaslin press being loaded at Piper Sonoma. This hand-loaded basket press has a capacity of eight tons, and is the same as the type used by Piper-Heidsieck in the Champagne region of France. Rather than crushing the grapes, it gently presses them.*

PRESTON VINEYARDS

Now maintaining over 120 acres of vineyard in the Dry Creek Valley of the Sonoma region, Preston Vineyards started out with just four acres of mature vines. In 1975, Louis Preston produced 500 cases wine; current production is 5,000 cases annually, with plans to increase production to 12,000 cases in the coming years. Growth has been rapid at Preston Vineyards — a brand-new winery was built in 1982 — but the quality of the wine has remained at the same high level.

All Preston Vineyards wines are grown, produced and bottled on the estate. Sauvignon Blanc and Zinfandel take up the major portion of Preston production, although the vineyard also

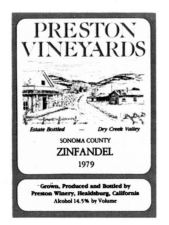

produces small case lots of Chenin Blanc, a Beaujolais-style Napa Gamay called Gamay Rouge and a generic white wine called Estate White. The 1979 Zinfandel is made in part from the older Zinfandel vines on the Preston ranch and has a special complexity, depth and richness. The 1981 Sauvignon Blanc has a defined varietal character. The winner of several awards, this wine has soft, herbaceous aromas and a honey-like texture.

QUAIL RIDGE WINERY

Quail Ridge aspires to be a winery in the finest chateau tradition. Founded in 1978, its cellar is located within the historic Hedgeside Caves in the Napa Valley, hand-hewn in 1883. The Chardonnay vineyards are located on Mt. Veeder and provide about half of the winery's needs; all other grapes, aside from a tiny amount of Pinot Noir, are purchased from Napa Valley growers. Production and distribution at Quail Ridge are very limited; only 52 cases of the 1980 Napa Valley Pinot Noir were made.

The 1982 French Colombard is a delightful dry white wine — soft, fruity and lightly balanced with oak, yet with uncommon depth and roundness. Quail Ridge makes two Chardonnays: Sonoma which is fresh, delicate and crisp, and Napa Valley which is rich, restrained and refined. The 1981 vintage of both is excellent.

MARTIN RAY VINEYARDS

Martin Ray, who died in 1976, is often called the father of the small premium winery in California. He was almost two decades ahead of his time when, in the 1940s, he planted varietals on top of 2,000-foot Mt. Eden in the Santa Clara area. His wines were handmade, vintage-dated and 100 percent varietal. Control of Martin Ray Vineyards remains in the family and the traditions carry on. Current production is about 4,000 cases of rather expensive wine.

The 1981 Dutton Ranch Chardonnay, just released, is a fine example of quality winemaking. Toasty, yet with a firm acid base, this wine is intensely flavorful. Also intense and deeply flavorful is the 1980 Steltzner Vineyard Cabernet Sauvignon; Merlot from 1979 is the same. Pinot Noir from the 1979 vintage at Winery Lake vineyard is strong, smooth and solid.

RAYMOND VINEYARD AND CELLAR

The Raymond Vineyard and Cellar was founded less than a decade ago but its beginnings go back half a century. In 1933, at the end of Prohibition, Roy Raymond, Sr. went to work at Beringer Vineyards. He served as winemaker until 1970. His sons, Roy, Jr. and Walt, also worked at Beringer — Roy as vineyard manager and Walt as assistant winemaker. When the Beringer family was forced to sell the winery in 1970, the Raymonds purchased 90 acres of land south of St. Helena and set up on their own.

Since receiving their bond in 1974, the Raymonds have produced a series of fine wines from their own grapes. The vineyard acreage is about 30 acres of Cabernet, 10 of Johannisberg Riesling and five each of Chenin Blanc and Merlot, with

The president of Ridge Vineyards is seen here (BELOW) *testing the sugar content of the grapes with a refractometer. This is a handy little device which will enable the vintner to decide when the grapes should be picked. It can also be used at a later stage in the winemaking process, to keep control of the level of sugar in the wine. Once the grapes have been picked they are often lightly crushed and de-stemmed before going into the fermenting vats.* (RIGHT) *Here, the Zinfandel, for which Ridge Vineyards are famous, is being pumped over in the fermenter tank.*

the balance in Chardonnay. The Raymonds are now producing about 40,000 cases a year, concentrating on Cabernet Sauvignon and Chardonnay, with highly regarded results. The goal of the Raymond Vineyard is to produce wines that are soft enough to be enjoyable while young, but that also age well. They have succeeded well recently, particularly with their 1980 Chardonnay and late harvest Johannisberg Rieslings.

RIDGE VINEYARDS

One of California's older wineries, Ridge Vineyards was founded in 1959 and released its first wines in 1962. The winery looks out over the Santa Clara Valley from Monte Bello Ridge in the Coast Range. Ridge pioneered in making wines from other areas and in specifying the vineyard on the label. Monte Bello is the winery's home vineyard. Cabernet grapes also come from York Creek vineyard on Spring Mountain in the Napa Valley; other grapes are purchased from selected premium vineyards. The winemaker is Paul Draper, one of the most highly regarded figures in the California wine industry. His reputation is based on the consistently magnificent wines he produces, using traditional methods. To keep the quality high, Draper keeps the quantity produced low. Total production is about 40,000 cases a year, with no plans to increase the amount.

The name Ridge is practically synonymous with Zinfandel and Cabernet Sauvignon, although the winery does produce some Petite Sirah and a tiny amount of Chardonnay. Ridge Zinfandels are big, intense wines, with remarkable aging potential. The Ridge practice of bottling and labeling by vineyard means that nine different, but equally excellent, Zinfandels are currently available. Ridge's best Cabernet comes from the Monte Bello vineyard. The 1977 release was outstanding; the 1979 York Creek Cabernet, just released, is also very fine.

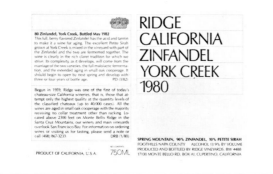

ROUDON-SMITH VINEYARDS

For the Smith and Roudon families, the dream of a vineyard and winery became reality in 1972, when they bought a site high up in the Santa Cruz Mountains of Scotts Valley. A small Chardonnay vineyard was planted and, that fall, 18 tons of purchased grapes were crushed and fermented.

By 1976, the tiny basement winery could not supply the increasing demand. A new winery building was completed in August of 1978 and the production goal of 10,000 cases a year was reached in 1981. From its inception, Roudon-Smith has sought out individual vineyards capable of providing the basis for the finest of varietal wines. Each of these vineyards is always identified by name on the label.

Production is currently centered around Chardonnay, Cabernet Sauvignon and Zinfandel. A Pinot Noir will be released when a vineyard that meets the Roudon-Smith standard of quality is found. To mark its 10th anniversary, Roudon-Smith Anniversary Selection labels display ancient wine-related implements and utensils.

ROUND HILL VINEYARDS

Despite its name, Round Hill Vineyards owns no vines. Instead, the winery buys grapes from Napa Valley growers, and also acts as a negotiant wine buyer. This means that the winery buy wines from other wineries for bottling under its own label. Round Hill has been in business since 1977 and now produces about 20,000 cases of premium Napa Valley wines each year. It has a solid reputation for high quality at modest prices.

Under the Rutherford Ranch label, Round Hill offers four vintage-dated varietals in limited quantities. The 1978 Napa Valley Late Harvest Zinfandel took a gold medal at an Orange County Fair, as did the 1978 Cabernet Sauvignon. Chardonnay and Sauvignon Blanc from Rutherford Ranch are also very good value.

RUTHERFORD HILL WINERY

On a wooded slope in the Napa Valley's east hills, the buildings of Rutherford Hill Winery pay modern architectural tribute to the fine wooden barns that were the valley's earliest distinctive buildings. Inside, the cellar blends innovation and tradition in the use of jacketed stainless steel tanks for winemaking and classic French oak barrels for aging.

Managing partners Charles Carpy and Bill Jaeger own most of the vineyards providing grapes to Rutherford Hill. Since its establishment in 1976, the winery has gained acclaim for both red and white wines. Marketing 85,000 cases annually, the winery will soon be producing over 100,000 cases a year. Top among the whites is the lovely, full-bodied Chardonnay; a fine, almost dry Gewürztraminer and a fruity Johannisberg Riesling are also available. The first release of Sauvignon Blanc, from young vines in Rutherford, was recently successfully made. First among the red wines is the rich Cabernet Sauvignon and the berry-like Merlot. A full-bodied Pinot Noir, very well-received, is made from grapes grown on Curtis Ranches' vineyard. Finally, Rutherford Hill produces a robust, unique Zinfandel from the fruit of 40-year-old vines at Giles Mead's Ranch on Atlas Peak, east of Napa.

ABOVE *The rustic yet contemporary wooden winery at Rutherford Hill is perched on a hillside overlooking the Silverado Trail in the east hills of the Napa Valley. Its large picnic area offers one of the best views of the vineyards and wineries of the Rutherford area.*

RUTHERFORD VINTNERS

After retiring from a prestigious winery as vice president in 1976, Bernard Skoda began Rutherford Vintners the same year. The winery became operational in 1977 and now produces about 15,000 cases a year. The grapes come chiefly from Skoda's own vineyards in the Napa Valley.

Rutherford Vintners' red wines have a distinctive varietal character, with delicately balanced acidity, tannin and oak. The primary wine,

At Rutherford Hill Winery in the Napa Valley, technological advances are applied to traditional winemaking methods. A mechanical harvester (FAR LEFT) is used to pick grapes quickly, when they are at the peak of ripeness. The juice pours out of the crusher and into fermentation tanks (LEFT). The wine is made in stainless steel tanks and aged in wooden casks (ABOVE).

Cabernet Sauvignon, is aged for three years in oak, one year in the bottle and only released for sale in the fifth year. The Chateau Rutherford Special Reserve Cabernet is made every year in limited quanitites, using grapes from a favored part of the winery's Rutherford vineyard. Pinot Noir is made in small amounts and is aged in French oak for as long as the Cabernet. A small amount of Merlot is also made each year and released after aging for three and a half years. Johannisberg Riesling is the second major wine produced at Rutherford Vintners. Made in the Rhine Kabinett style with a slight amount of botrytis, it has a rich, full flavor. The first release of Chardonnay was in 1982; it is in the classic dry and crisp style.

ST. CLEMENT VINEYARDS

The winery at St. Clement Vineyards is located in the historic, 1876 mansion of the owner, Dr. William J. Casey. The Casey family bought the property in the Napa Valley in 1975, and now produce about 6,000 cases a year, mostly of Pinot Chardonnay and Cabernet Sauvignon. Small amounts of Sauvignon Blanc are just becoming available and more is on the way.

Although on the expensive side the 1979 St. Clement Cabernet Sauvignon is worth the price. Strongly tannic and fruity, this wine will improve well with bottle aging. The 1980 Chardonnay has been well received; it too is quite expensive. The recently released 1981 Sauvignon Blanc is complex and attractive. It is made in a light, fresh style, with a crisp finish.

SANFORD & BENEDICT VINEYARDS

Because the Sanford & Benedict Vineyards is located only a few miles from the Pacific Ocean, in the Santa Ynez Valley of Santa Barbara County, the climate in the summer is very cool. This provides the ideal conditions for Burgundian grape varieties and more than half of the vineyard's 110 acres are planted to Pinot Noir and Chardonnay. Partners J. Richard Sanford and Michael Benedict purchased the property in 1972 and built their winery in 1976. They produce wines using traditional French techniques, including fining with egg whites, and they age their wines in barrels for longer than is usual. The result is 10,000 cases a year of exceptionally fine estate-grown and estate-bottled wines.

Sanford & Benedict specializes in Pinot Noirs that are deeply complex and intense, with a perceptible French style. The Chardonnay is smooth and pure, again with a French touch. An interesting wine from Sanford & Benedict is Tintillón, a proprietory name for a light Pinot Noir. This wine is made just like Chardonnay, using white wine techniques; it is pale pink and has a dry, fruity taste. Cabernet Sauvignon is made without refrigeration and is consequently very deep in color and rich in flavor.

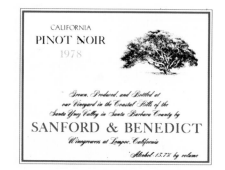

SAN MARTIN WINERY

In an early example of cooperative winemaking in the Santa Clara area, the original San Martin winery was built in 1908. Until Prohibition, which forced its closure, the cooperative produced jug wines. After Prohibition, the winery was purchased by the Bruno Felice family who then developed it further. Several ownership changes followed and now San Martin Winery is owned by the Somerset Wine Company. Since 1977, the winery has advanced in the area of premium varietal wines. The winemaking facility is one of the most modern in the California wine industry and turns out more than 80,000 cases each year.

Among the wines produced by San Martin, several stand out. Cabernet Sauvignon is soft with mild pepper overtones and the Chenin Blanc has a full, ripe flavor. Grapes with exceptional potential are used to make San Martin Special Reserve wines. Recent releases under this label include Chardonnay and Fumé Blanc from 1980 and Cabernet Sauvignon from 1978. An interesting concept from San Martin is "soft" wines with a low alcohol content. The 1980 Soft Chenin Blanc is now available.

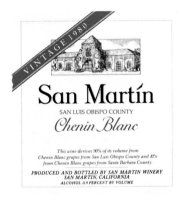

SANTA CRUZ MOUNTAIN VINEYARD

The speciality of Santa Cruz Mountain Vineyard is Pinot Noir, the most temperamental of California varietals. Owner Ken Burnap attracted a lot of attention with is first Pinot Noir in 1975 and his reputation has been growing ever since. So has his winery — he now makes Cabernet Sauvignon and Chardonnay as well, although production is still limited to about 3,000 cases a year.

In general, Cabernet Sauvignon from Santa Cruz Mountain vineyard is very deep, with a lovely dark color and a lingering finish. The 1978 and 1979 releases are fine examples. The Chardonnay is made in small amounts from three different vineyards and is still experimental. The famous Pinot Noirs of Santa Cruz are not easily found, but worth searching for. The 1977 release has an intense nose; it is full-bodied with lots of tannin and a long finish. It also won almost every competition of that year. The 1978/1979 release is equally good, with perfect balance.

SANTINO WINERY

Located in the heart of Amador County, Santino Winery produces fine wines from grapes grown exclusively in the Shenandoah Valley. Santino has no vineyards of its own, but the winery, established in 1979, has already won a number of awards, especially for its Zinfandels. The Shenandoah Valley Zinfandel is a *cuvée* of three vineyards, with a berry aroma, a hint of French oak and the chocolate finish distinctive of the region. The 1979 vintage took a gold medal at the 1981 Los Angeles County Fair. Grapes from the 70-year-old Eschen Vineyard are used to make Fiddletown Zinfandel, known for its raspberry-like aroma and peppery snap. Santino's White Harvest Zinfandel is light and fresh, with a clean aroma and a strong, fruity taste. The 1981 vintage has been placed highly in competition.

The 1982 Late Harvest Riesling, made from completely botrytized grapes, is the result of unusual growing conditions and is excellent.

SCHRAMSBERG VINEYARDS

High on the western slopes of the Napa Valley, Schramsberg Vineyards was founded in 1862 by Jacob Schram. Although successful in Schram's lifetime, the vineyard gradually fell into idleness after his death in 1905. In 1965 Jack and Jamie Davies purchased the estate and began restoring the cellars as one of the world's premier producers of bottle-fermented sparkling wine. The Davies grow Chardonnay, Pinot Noir and Pinot Blanc grapes in the hillside vineyards. These grapes, together with Gamay and Flora from selected growers in the Napa Valley, are used to produce five distinct styles of sparkling wine. Reserve (Brut) is made from select wines of each vintage, and is aged over four years before being

LEFT *The homestead of Jack and Jamie Davies, the owners of Schramsberg Vineyards, is situated near Calistogo in the Napa Valley. The Davies purchased the vineyards in 1965 in a delapidated state, but have built them up to produce some of California's best champagne-type wines. Sparkling wines are fermented in vats (*TOP*) for a limited period before being transferred to bottles, where further fermentation can be controlled. The wine is checked for sediment periodically (*ABOVE*).*

released. Blanc de Blancs (Brut) is a light, austere *cuvée* of Chardonnay and Pinot Blanc; Blanc de Noirs (Brut) is a complex, rich blend of Pinot Noir and Chardonnay. The Cuvée de Pinot (Brut) is a spicy, fruity *cuvée* made from a blend of Pinot Noir and Napa Gamay, and the Cremant (Demi-sec) is a unique, less effervescent dessert wine made primarily from Flora grapes.

Schramsberg sparkling wines are marketed in limited quantities in 28 states and a number of foreign markets. In 1982 production capacity was developed to 50,000 cases.

SEBASTIANI VINEYARDS

The first vineyard to be planted north of San Francisco was at the Mission de Sonoma in 1825. The padres would use the grapes to make altar wine; today, their vineyards are next to the binning cellars at Sebastiani Vineyards. The current winery was founded in 1904 by Samuele Sebastiani, who was an Italian immigrant. It remains a family concern, with third-generation Sam J. Sebastiani in charge. The winery now produces about 4,000,000 cases of wine each year, mostly generic and jug wines under the August Sebastiani label. The Sebastiani Vineyards label appears on Premium wines and Proprietor's Reserve wines. Since 1982, all premium varietal wines have been vintage-dated and it is likely that future wines will be excellent.

Among the interesting fine white wines from Sebastiani are "Eye of the Swan" Pinot Noir Blanc, with a pale, coppery hue, and Green Hungarian, which is light gold with a greenish cast. Among the red wines is the "Nouveau" Gamay Beaujolais, which was made for the first time in 1972, the first in the United States. "Tailfeathers" Pinot Noir Trés Rouge is very deep in color and intense in flavor.

SHAFER VINEYARDS

Shafer Vineyards was officially founded in 1979. The story really begins in 1972, however, when John Shafer, an executive in a Chicago publishing firm, changed careers and brought his wife and four children to the Napa Valley. Here the family purchased a neglected, 50-year-old vineyard in the eastern foothills, at the northern tip of the Stag's Leap palisades. Within a year they began the arduous task of ripping out the old vines, fumigating and terracing the hillsides, installing irrigation systems and replanting 40 acres.

The family's decision to make their own wine came from the vineyard's location and the grape varietals they had planted. The Stag's Leap area, with its unique microclimate and rocky, hilly terrain, is ideal for Cabernet Sauvignon. Shafer Vineyards' first release, in 1981, was a 1978 Cabernet having an intense character, dark color, extreme richness and a very long finish. The family plans to produce approximately 12,000 cases annually, divided among Cabernet, Zinfandel and Chardonnay. All their wines are allowed to clarify by themselves, since the Shafers feel that filtration intrudes on the natural winemaking process.

SHOWN & SONS VINEYARDS

The Shown family has been growing grapes in their Vinedo de las Aguacitas (Vineyard by the Little Waters) in the Napa Valley since 1973. The winery's first crush was in 1979, when the first Shown & Sons premium estate-bottled varietals were produced. The winery now makes 15,000 cases a year.

The Showns started well with their 1979 Cabernet Sauvignon, a rich wine with intense varietal flavors. The 1980 version is soft and warm in the mouth, with deep, dark color. The first bottling of Zinfandel was in 1980, and resulted in a wine that has a classic raspberry-like taste. The 1981 release has a slightly peppery nose and mouth-filling warmth. The 1981 Chenin Blanc is dry, with just a touch of natural sweetness, as is the 1981 Johannisberg Riesling. Shown & Sons uses a blend of 60 percent Johannisberg Riesling and 40 percent Chenin Blanc to makes it proprietary wine, Johannisberg Blanc. The flavor combines Riesling fruitiness with Chenin Blanc dryness to create a pleasantly light table wine.

SIERRA VISTA WINERY

A tiny, premium winery in El Dorado County, Sierra Vista is located on a ridge 2,800 feet high, looking out over the Crystal range of the Sierra Nevada Mountains. John and Barbara MacReady began operations in 1977. The 27 acres of vineyard are planted to Cabernet Sauvignon, Chardonnay, Sauvignon Blanc and Zinfandel. Additional grapes, particularly Zinfandel, are purchased from small, locally owned vineyards. In 1982 Sierra Vista made 2,500 cases of wine. The MacReadys expect to reach the 5,000-case level in the near future and plan to stay as small as is financially possible.

BELOW *The owners of Sierra Vista Winery, John and Barbara MacCreedy, inspect Cabernet Sauvignon vines in their 27-acre vineyard at El Dorado County.*

Cabernet Sauvignon from Sierra Vista is stored for 20 months in small oak cooperage and then bottle-aged for one year before release. Oak barrels are used to complete fermentation for the Chardonnays, giving them a smooth, buttery flavor that balances the fruitiness of local grapes. Zinfandel is quite reasonably priced; 1978 is a particularly good release. Sierra Vista also makes Sauvigon Blanc and White Zinfandel and a very aromatic Chenin Blanc.

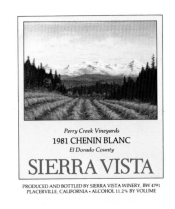

SIMI WINERY

The Simi Winery roots go back to Guiseppe and Pietro Simi, who founded the winery in the Alexander Valley in 1881. Both brothers died in 1904, leaving Guiseppe's teenaged daughter Isabelle to carry on. She did so, successfully running the firm until its sale in 1970. Through several subsequent changes of ownership, Isabelle remained involved with the winery until her death in 1981. Simi

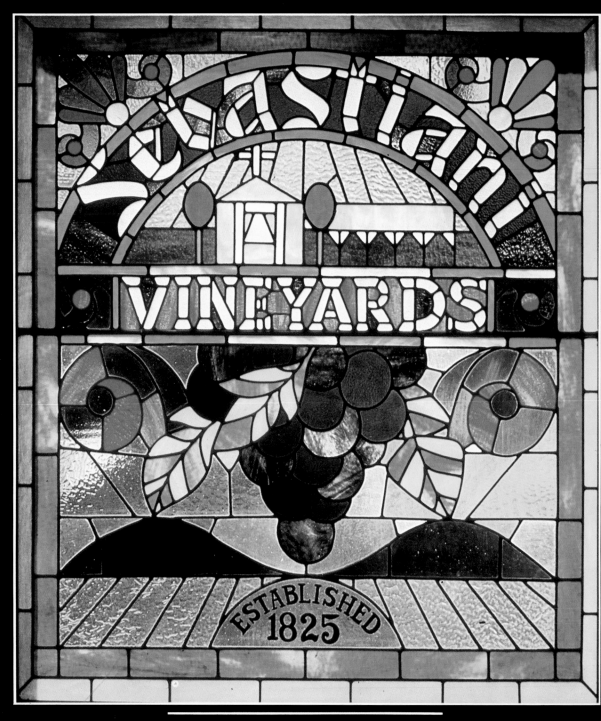

This stained-glass window at the Sebastiani Vineyards winery (ABOVE) commemorates the founding of the original vineyards on the site which happened in 1825. This was the beginning of winemaking in northern California. The largest collection of hand-carved wine casks in America is on display in the winery.

Winery is now owned by Möet-Hennessy, France's largest wine and spirits company. More than half of Simi's total production of 140,000 cases annually is Chardonnay and Cabernet Sauvignon. The winemaker is Zelma Long, who is highly respected for her technical and practical expertise. She is also a partner in Long Vineyards, a small, highly regarded winery in the Napa Valley.

Simi's 1980 Mendocino County Chardonnay has subtle oak flavors and a buttery, rich texture. It is extremely well balanced. The 1978 Cabernet Sauvignon from the Alexander Valley is smooth and harmonious. The substantial acid and alcohol moderate the tannin to create a softly drinkable wine. Although it is only a small part of its production, Gewürztraminer from Simi Valley is consistently outstanding.

After crushing, the juice and skins of white grapes at Simi Winery are kept together for up to 24 hours in the skin contact tower, shown (LEFT). A gravity-fed press below the tower gently extracts additional juice from the skins without adding bitterness or astringency. Simi's magnificent hand-hewn stone winery (BELOW) was built in 1890 by the winery's founders, the Italian immigrant brothers Pietro and Giuseppe Simi. Now owned by Moet-Hennessy, Simi is one of the best-equipped facilities in the industry.

SMITH-MADRONE VINEYARDS AND WINERY

At an altitude of 1,700 feet on famed Spring Mountain, the Smith-Madrone Vineyards provide spectacular views of the Napa Valley below. This small, highly rated vineyard was begun in 1971, when the land was purchased and timbering started. The first vines were planted in 1972, with about 20 acres equally divided among Cabernet Sauvignon, Pinot Noir, Johannisberg Riesling and Chardonnay. The plantings now cover about 40 acres, with plans to expand gradually to 50.

All Smith-Madrone wines are made only from their own grapes. In 1977, their first crush produced 300 cases of Johannisberg Riesling. This wine subsequently won first place in the prestigious Riesling division of the Gault-Millau Wine Olympiad in Paris. Smith-Madrone's Pinot Noirs, Chardonnays and Cabernet Sauvignons have recently come on the market. They are all excellent, the only problem being their limited supply. Smith-Madrone makes fewer than 5,000 cases a year and most of that is sold by mailing lists or at the winery. Small quantities are available at retail wine shops in California and the 1981 Riesling can be found nationally at discerning wine dealers.

SONOMA VINEYARDS

In 1962, Rodney Strong bought a small winery in Sonoma County and almost immediately began making highly regarded wines. He prospered and Sonoma Vineyards now grows and harvests its 13 vintaged wines from over 1,600 acres of estate-designated vineyards. In addition to varietal table wines, Sonoma produces Champagnes as part of a joint venture with Piper Heidsieck of France. Not counting Champagne, the winery has a capacity of 3,400,000 gallons. In 1982, Sonoma Vineyards won a total of 18 awards in just three significant wine judgings. Small batches of especially promising grapes are estate-bottled and designated by a special gold-script label.

Cabernet Sauvignon with the Alexander's Crown designation is a big wine, with a mouth-filling body. It is consistently excellent. The Zinfandel from the River West Vineyard, made from the fruit of very old wines, is full-flavored, with an intense berry-like taste. Also from the River West vineyard is a fruity, flinty Chardonnay.

SOTOYOME WINERY

The original land grant of Rancho Sotoyome was made in 1840 and covered 48,000 acres. The current winery is located in the Russian River Valley on 10 acres of the old rancho. It draws its grapes from its own vineyard and from selected small vineyards in the area. A small, family-run operation, Sotoyome Winery made its first crush in 1974. The present production is about 2,000 cases a year, with no immediate plans for expansion beyond 3,000 cases.

Chardonnay is the only white wine made at Sotoyome. The grapes of the 1981 vintage came from the Dry Creek Valley, and made a wine that has medium body and relatively high acid, with some oak and full varietal flavors. The grapes used for Zinfandel come from Soyotome's own vineyard. The 1982 release is full-bodied with a lively, fruity flavor. The 1979 Petite Sirah is completely dry and is an excellent, deep-colored, robust table wine. Sotoyome's 1979 Cabernet Sauvignon is also made from grapes which are grown in the Dry Creek Valley. It is a brightly-colored wine, with medium-body and is a classic example of California Cabernet.

SOUVERAIN

The winery at Souverain is owned by the North Coast Grape Growers Association, a partnership of approximately 250 grape growers in the famed California North Coast counties. Since the winery's purchase in 1976 from Pillsbury, all Souverain wines carry the designation "North Coast Appellation." Annual production is over 500,000 cases.

Souverain produces a full line of premium varietal, vintage-dated wines from grapes grown predominantly in Sonoma, Napa and Mendocino Counties. The white wines include the complex, dry, oak-aged Chardonnay and Fumé Blanc, the crisp Chablis, the delightful semi-dry Grey Riesling, Johannisberg Riesling, Gewürztraminer, Chenin Blanc, and Colombard Blanc, and the fragrant, fruity dessert wine, Muscat Canelli. Souverain's award-winning rosé is made from Pinot Noir grapes. The list of red wines begins with the light, youthful, fruity Gamay Beaujolais. It also includes dry-fermented, oak-aged Petite Sirah, Charbono, Cabernet Sauvignon, Merlot, Burgundy, Pinot Noir and Zinfandel. Wines of exceptional merit are designated with the Vintage Selection label. An estate-bottling program is just beginning and looks promising.

The unusual design of the showcase winery at Souverain (ABOVE) *was inspired by the many old hopkilns that can still be seen around the countryside of Sonoma County.*

SPRING MOUNTAIN VINEYARDS

The restored 1885 mansion at Spring Mountain Vineyards is the home of the vineyard owner Mike Robbins, and is also the mansion used in the CBS television series "Falcon Crest." Many of the outdoor scenes are filmed among Spring Mountain's vineyards, but it was not television that made this winery famous. Founded in 1968, it now produces about 25,000 cases of finely crafted varietals each year. Distribution is throughout 41 states and seven countries. Some grapes come from the 35 acres of vines planted near the winery; the remainder come from vineyards owned by Robbins elsewhere in the Napa Valley.

The Spring Mountain 1979 Cabernet Sauvignon stands out as does the 1980 Chardonnay. Sauvignon Blanc at Spring Mountain is character-

ized by a steely, gunmetal taste; the 1980 release is wonderfully dry. The 1981 Sauvignon Blanc combines considerable depth and complexity in the aromas with crispness and delicacy in the flavors. The third release to appear under Spring Mountain's Falcon Crest label is a zesty, fruity, 1981 Gamay Beaujolais. Quite reasonably priced, this wine represents excellent value.

ABOVE *In the winery at Spring Mountain Vineyards, the stainless steel fermenting vats and the horizontal press are right next to each other. This allows a minimum of undesirable oxidation to occur.*

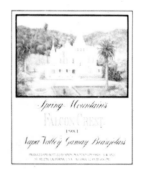

*The mansion at Spring Mountain Vineyards has been
restored to its 1885 splendor (LEFT). The inset shows
one of the employees license plates. Owner Mike Robbins
inspects barrels in his unusual cellar (TOP), which has a
stained-glass window (ABOVE).*

STAG'S LEAP WINE CELLARS

The 1973 Cabernet Sauvignon from Stag's Leap Wine Cellars took first place in a famed international tasting held in Paris in 1976. The wine was made from owner Warren Winiarski's third harvest; later vintages have consistently equalled or excelled that standard. The 45-acre vineyard is located on the floor of the Napa Valley, on the eastern side along the Silverado Trail. It is planted mostly to Cabernet Sauvignon and Merlot. Grapes for other wines are purchased from carefully supervised growers in the region.

Stag's Leap is noted for powerful Cabernet Sauvignons with intense varietal flavor. The Chardonnays are also famed for their body and classic flavor. Made to the same standard of excellence is Johannisberg Riesling.

BELOW *Skillful cellar work is needed so that the wine stacked in barrels at Stag's Leap Wine Cellars remains in good condition. The barrels should not be moved until the wine is ready for bottling.*

P. AND M. STAIGER WINERY

The winery at P. and M. Staiger is at an elevation of 1,100 feet in the Santa Cruz Mountains. Two vineyards totaling five acres are in two south-facing bowls below the winery. The Staiger family began making wine here in 1973. The vineyards were planted in 1975 with Chardonnay and in an 80-20 percent mix with Cabernet Sauvignon and Merlot. All Staiger wines are estate-grown, with production at a steady 1,000 gallons a year.

The 1980 Chardonnay was the second harvest from Staiger's own vines. It has the intense flavor characteristic of mountain-grown grapes.

ROBERT STEMMLER WINERY

When it began production in 1977, the Robert Stemmler Winery made just 1,000 cases of Chardonnay. Applying his extensive training in the German wine industry, owner Robert Stemmler has now expanded output to 7,000 cases produced at the winery in Dry Creek Valley.

Current releases from Stemmler include an award-winning 1979 Chardonnay that is rich and elegant; the Cabernet Sauvignon from 1979, another winner, is complex and full-bodied. Fumé Blanc, also from 1979, is dry with a subtle fruit flavor. Stemmler has just added a Pinot Noir. In addition to premium wines under the Robert Stemmler label, a secondary label called Bel Canto has just been released. The 1978 Cabernet Sauvignon is a reasonably priced wine, but is also of a high quality.

1979
SONOMA COUNTY
CHARDONNAY
Made and Bottled by
ROBERT STEMMLER WINES
GEYSERVILLE, CALIFORNIA
Alcohol 12.5% by Volume

STERLING VINEYARDS

Probably the most spectacular in the entire Napa Valley, the winery at Sterling Vineyards is reached by a cable car that carries visitors 300 feet up from the valley floor. The first parcels were acquired in 1964 and were originally privately held, although since 1977 The Coca-Cola Company (Atlanta) has owned the operation. Although Sterling Vineyards produces some 100,000 cases of wine a year, it still ranks as one of the larger "small" wineries in the area. All Sterling wines are estate-bottled.

In recent years Sterling has been concentrating on just four premium varietal wines: Cabernet Sauvignon, Merlot, Chardonnay and Sauvignon Blanc. The Cabernets have been especially well received, particularly those from 1978 and 1979,

The tasting rooms at Sterling Vineyards (BELOW) *offer shelter from the summer sun, which can affect the wine.*

which are well-structured and stylish. Sterling was a pioneer with Merlot, at one time having as much as 75 percent of the total Merlot acreage in California. The wine is fruity and rich. A Sauvignon Blanc from Sterling is dry and elegant, with a touch of wood from the small French cooperage. The best-known of Sterling's wines is probably Chardonnay. Consistently excellent, these wines are held for two years before release, and have a lovely bouquet of French oak.

STEVENOT WINERY

Located in the historic gold rush country of the Sierra Nevada foothills, Stevenot Winery is at an elevation of 1,800 feet with limestone-based soils. The winery was founded in 1978 by Barden Stevenot, a fifth-generation member of a pioneer family in Calaveras County. Current production is about 15,000 cases a year. About a quarter of the production comes from Stevenot's own vineyards, planted in Cabernet Sauvignon, Zinfandel, Chenin Blanc and, recently, Chardonnay. The remainder of the grapes come from selected vineyards located throughout California.

In the past few years Stevenot Winery has been awarded 14 medals at important California county fairs, especially for the 1979 Chardonnay and 1979 and 1980 Chenin Blancs.

Stevenot
1982
Amador County
Zinfandel-Blanc

STONEGATE WINERY

Stonegate Winery was founded in 1973 by James and Barbara Spaulding with the aim of producing premium varietal wines of exceptional quality. The winery is at the northern end of the Napa Valley, near the northern edge of the Mayacamas Mountains. From these hillside vineyards come Stonegate's Spaulding Vineyard Merlot and Spaulding Vineyard Chardonnay, as well as grapes for Stonegate's Napa Valley Cabernet

Winemaker Warren Winiarski of Stag's Leap Cellars transfers carbon dioxide from a fermenting tank of Chardonnay to one containing Pinot Noir (BELOW). The Pinot Noir has been fermenting for so long that it no longer produces its own carbon dioxide. After fermentation, the wines will be placed in Nevers oak casks for aging. The must from the red wine has to be pumped over during fermentation to break up the cap and ensure skin-juice contact. This tank of Pinot Noir (RIGHT) is being pumped over after fermenting for two weeks. Pumping over often occurs twice a day during the course of fermentation. The vigor and completeness with which this is done, however, depends on the nature of the grapes. Very rich grapes should be pumped over with restraint.

The winery at Sterling Vineyards is modeled after an early California mission (BOTTOM). Wines at Sterling are aged in French oak barrels from Nevers and Limousin (BELOW LEFT). The red wines are fermented in large oak tanks (BELOW RIGHT). Each tank is made of French oak and has a capacity of 3,000 gallons. White wines are fermented in stainless steel tanks.

After 10 years of growing fine grapes for other wineries, Leo and Evelyn Trentadue, along with their son, Victor, decided to make their own wines in 1969. Currently about a third of the grapes grown on their 200 acres in the upper Alexander Valley go into their wines; they continue to sell the rest. The Trentadues eventually hope to increase capacity so that all their grapes are used for their own wines. Production now is 20,000 cases a year.

Trentadue means "32" in Italian, and all Trentadue labels have this number on them. Among the fresh, young, fruity white wines are oak-aged Chardonnay, Sauvignon Blanc, French Colombard, Johannisberg Riesling and Chenin Blanc. The Trentadue reds are dry, natural, dinner wines, well-aged by three years in French and American oak casks. Among them are a complex Cabernet Sauvignon, a dynamic Early Burgundy, an award-winning Petite Sirah, a deep-hued Carignane, Merlot and flowery, elegant Gamay. Trentadue Zinfandels are always excellent; the 1976 vintage is an outstanding example. Aleatico, a spicy Italian dessert wine, is also produced by the Trentadue family.

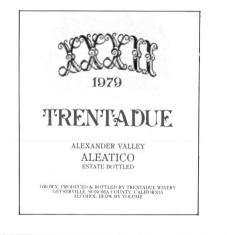

TURGEON & LOHR WINERY

Little more than 10 years after planting their first grapes, the Turgeon & Lohr Winery is one of the 100 largest in the country. The vineyards cover 280 acres of rich, loamy soil set in the cool coastal climate of Monterey County. Turgeon & Lohr wines are marketed under the J. Lohr label, and include their proprietary wine, JADE, a fruity, low-alcohol, white wine blend.

Because the climatic conditions are ideal, the J. Lohr Pinot Blanc is excellent, with a full bouquet of Limousin oak. Turgeon & Lohr also produce Chardonnay and Reserve Chardonnay (not every year), Fumé Blanc, Johannisberg Riesling and a small crop of Pinot Noir. The J. Lohr Monterey Gamay has been a consistent award-winner. Their Cabernet Sauvignon, aged in oak for 24 months, contains selected Napa Valley grapes.

In addition to their Monterey vineyards, Turgeon & Lohr grow Zinfandel, Chenin Blanc and Petite Sirah grapes at Clarksburg in the Sacramento River Delta region. Their Chenin Blanc has won several awards at prestigious tastings; the Petite Sirah is complex, full-bodied, yet soft on the palate.

VENTANA VINEYARD

The Ventana Vineyard is primarily a premium grape grower, supplying fine grapes to limited-production wineries. Owners Doug and Shirley Meador began making lots of varietal wines in 1978, and won almost instantaneous acclaim. Located on the west side of the Salinas Valley in Monterey County, Ventana has 305 acres of vineyards and an annual production that varies according to conditions. The goal is 25,000 cases.

The beautiful color photograph on the label of Ventana wines is changed each year. Regardless of the picture, Ventana wines stand out, particularly the whites. The Sauvignon Blanc is rich and heavy, with a fresh, fruity aroma. Ventana Chardonnay is intensely flavored with a golden color and exceptionally good balance, while the dry Chenin Blanc is flavorful and complex, with a touch of tartness. Among the red wines, Ventana Cabernet Sauvignon, Zinfandel and Petite Sirah are all excellent.

VILLA MT. EDEN

A century of history lies behind Villa St. Eden. Vineyards were first planted on the site on the current winery in 1881, the decade that saw the birth of the Napa Valley as a wine-producing region. The vineyards have been in continuous production over the years. In 1970 James and Anne McWilliams purchased the property, and have considerably upgraded it with new plantings and a modernized winery. Of the 87 acres that make up the ranch, 63 are planted in Cabernet Sauvignon, Chardonnay, Pinot Noir and Chenin Blanc. Some Gewürztraminer is also grown. In all, about 18,500 cases of estate-bottled wine are produced every year.

Villa St. Eden's 1974 Cabernet Sauvignon created a sensation when it was released, and later Cabernets have been equally fine. The 1979 Reserve Cabernet Sauvignon, for example, is exceptionally well-balanced. But Villa St. Eden also produces other wines including a charming 1980 Chardonnay, a crisp and fruity 1980 Chenin Blanc and a complex, fruity, and very good 1979 Pinot Noir. One of only a handful of California wineries to produce an Alsatian-style dry Gewürztraminer, Villa St. Eden's 1981 vintage is delightful with a flowery bouquet.

WENTE BROS.

The Wente Bros. tradition of winemaking dates back four generations, to 1883 and Carl H. Wente. Arriving in California from Germany, Carl founded his first vineyards on 50 acres in the gravelly Livermore Valley. He prospered, and two of his sons, Ernest and Herman, continued in the family business. Following the end of Prohibition in 1934, the brothers were among the first to put a varietal label on their wine bottles. Ernest's son Karl became winemaker in 1961, following in his uncle's footsteps. Karl was among the first vintners to recognize the potential of Monterey County for growing premium wine grapes, and expanded the family vineyards into that area in 1962. The Monterey vineyards, at the mouth of the Arroyo Seco, have grown to 600 acres, while the home vineyards in Livermore now cover 850 acres. Today, Wente Bros. produces nearly 720,000 cases a year of 14 different wines.

From the beginning, the emphasis at Wente Bros. has been on white wines. The winery is the largest producer of Grey Riesling in the United States. Among the other fine whites are Dry Semillon, Pinot Blanc, Sauvignon Blanc and Johannisberg Riesling. The Wentes released their first sparkling wine in 1983, a 1980 vintage Brut.

WOODBURY WINERY

The art of producing fine port wine has been triumphantly brought to California by Russ and Linda Woodbury, owners of Woodbury Winery. Their first vintage was in 1977, and although it is years before the ultimate success of a particular port vintage can be gauged, they must already limit buyers to one case each.

The Woodburys adhere mostly to tradition in making their port. There is no fining or filtration, for example, so Woodbury ports must be decanted before drinking. In addition, they follow the Portuguese practice of using 160°-179° proof brandy to fortify the wine, rather than the higher-proof, more neutral spirits used by other makers. Where the Woodburys break from tradition is in their choice of grapes. They favor grapes from older, hillside vineyards, as do the Portuguese, but they use the Cabernet Sauvignon, Petite Sirah and Zinfandel grapes of California's north coast, rather than seeking grapes that resemble those of Portugal. The 1977 harvest yielded fewer than 600 cases; the winery's maximum capacity is 4,000 cases a year.

The Woodburys have also penetrated another European mystery — fine cognac in the French style. Woodbury Winery now offers double-distilled brandy made from Saint-Emilion grapes. Aged in American oak, this brandy has a full, round character ideal for after-dinner sipping.

ZACA MESA WINERY

The first vineyards at Zaca Mesa were planted on mesas overlooking the Santa Ynez Valley in 1972. They now total 220 acres, with an additional 120 acres near Santa Maria. The production of estate-bottled, award-winning wines is now 80,000 cases a year. The goal of owner Marshall Ream is to establish an American estate making premium wines. To that end, he specializes in six varietals: Johannisberg Riesling, Chardonnay, Sauvignon Blanc, Pinot Noir, Zinfandel and Cabernet Sauvignon. All varietals made by Zaca Mesa have earned gold medals over the years in major California competitions.

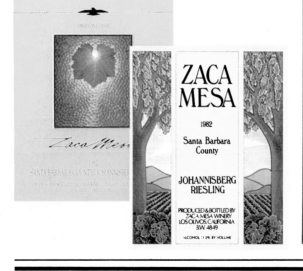

Specially selected and vinified lots of wine are produced in limited quantities at Zaca Mesa under the American Estate designation. Two outstanding wines were recently released with this label — a rich, intense 1979 Cabernet Sauvignon and an elegant, strongly varietal Chardonnay from 1981.

RIGHT *Zaca Mesa's winery and vineyards, overlooking the Santa Ynez Valley, are on land that was once part of the Spanish grant called "La Zaca." An Indian word,* zaca *means peaceful or tranquil.*

ZD WINES

ZD Wines is a small, two-family winery, founded in 1969 by the two partners whose initials form its name — Gino Zepponi and Norman deLeuze. From the first 350 cases they and their families produced in 1969 at their small winery in Sonoma, their crush steadily increased until they built a new facility in Napa in 1979. They currently produce about 9,000 cases per year. Norman deLeuze manages the winery full-time, with his son Robert as assistant winemaker.

Using classic methods of winemaking, ZD produces primarily Chardonnay and Pinot Noir, although increasing amounts of Cabernet Sauvignon are being produced. Merlot, Zinfandel and White Riesling are also being made. The ZD Wines philosophy is to produce wines with a minimum of intervention and a maximum of personal attention. The result is full-bodied, full-flavored wines that display the varietal character of each one as much as possible. Recently, of 15 entries of Chardonnay, Cabernet Sauvignon and Pinot Noir in wine competitions, 12 medals were won. The 1979 Chardonnay was served on state occasions at the White House in 1982.

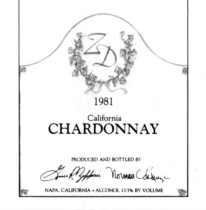

THE WINES OF
NEW YORK

The wine industry of New York state is the second largest in America. The state has been famous since the start of the nineteenth century for wines made from its native grapes, including Concord, Catawba, and Niagara. Since the turn of the century, French hybrid grapes with much less of the characteristic foxiness of American native grapes have been successfully grown. More recently, since the mid-1970s, varietal vinifera grapes have become an important part of the state's winemaking.
There are three main wine-producing regions of New York: the Finger Lakes, the Hudson Valley and the North Fork of Long Island.

The Finger Lakes The Finger Lakes region is in northern New York, east of Buffalo and close to Lake Ontario. The hilly slopes along these long, thin lakes experience very cold winters and a long, sunny growing season. The region is on the same latitude as the major wine regions of France. Historically, this is one of the oldest wine-producing regions in the country. Taylor and Great Western are there, located in Hammondsport on Keuka Lake. Among other vineyards in the area are Bully Hill, Glenora, Chateau Esperanza and Merman Wiemer. Other lakes are Seneca, Cayuga and Canandaigua.

Hudson River A fairly new region, the Hudson River area is about 50 miles north of New York City. It is hilly, with milder winters than the Finger Lakes region. The area has gained some fame for its hybrid wines, particularly Seyval Blanc. Vineyards in the area include Benmarl, Clinton and North Salem. This is definitely an area to watch.

North Fork The rural North Fork is at the eastern tip of Long Island, about 80 miles due east of New York City. The climate is moderate and the soil excellent for vinifera varietals. Although there is evidence that grapes were grown in the area in the late seventeenth century, the first vineyard to be planted in recent memory was Hargrave, in 1973. A few have followed and more are sure to realize the area's potential.

BENMARL VINEYARDS

Benmarl Vineyards may well be the oldest continuously operated vineyard in the east and possibly in America. The present vineyards were once known as the Caywood Vineyard, which was originally planted in 1867. The property was purchased by Mark Miller in 1957 and replanted over a period of 15 years in 20 acres of French varietals and French hybrids. Construction on the winery began in 1969; it was licensed in 1971. To finance experimentation and research in the pursuit of excellence, and to encourage interest in Hudson River region wines, Miller created the Société des Vignerons, whose members purchase the "vineright" to two grape vines. Vignerons receive a case of wine with special labels, may purchase limited-production wines and may participate in the harvest. The membership has grown to over 1,000. Annual production at Benmarl is about 7,500 cases a year. Benmarl red and white table wines are available to the general public and the majority are excellent.

BRIMSTONE HILL VINEYARD

Located in the southeastern foothills of the Shawangunk Mountains, in the middle of the Hudson River region, Brimstone Hill aims to produce wines with a French character. In 1969 four acres of vineyards were planted with French hybrids. Red wines from Brimstone Hill are light-bodied and age well in the bottle; the white wines have a distinctive, delicate flavor and are good for young drinking. Blends from Brimstone Hill include Hudson River Region (HRR) Red Table Wine, HRR White Table Wine and HRR Rosé Table Wine. The only varietal wine made is New York State Aurore. All Brimstone Hill wines are vintage-dated and estate-bottled.

BULLY HILL VINEYARDS

The owner, winemaker and label artist of Bully Hill Vineyards is Walter S. Taylor, grandson of Walter Taylor, who founded The Taylor Wine Company. Since 1976, Bully Hill Vineyards and Walter S. Taylor have not been connected with or successors to The Taylor Wine Company that is now owned by The Coca-Cola Company of Atlanta, Georgia. The fascinating labels used by Bully Hill call the wines by some unusual names, such as Red Rooster and Love My Goat, both red wines, and Space Shuttle, a rosé. However, despite the fun names the contents are to be taken seriously. Fourteen varieties of French hybrid grapes are grown at Bully Hill Vineyards, which is located 1,000 feet above Lake Keuka in the Finger Lakes region. The New York State varietal and sparkling wines are excellent and the various generic blends are thoughtfully and carefully produced. All Bully Hill wines are additive-free and are estate-bottled and the owner insists that only New York State grapes are used.

CAGNASSO WINERY

The tiny Cagnasso Winery began operations with the vintage of 1977. At most, when the harvest is good, 6,000 gallons of wine are made in a year. Located in the historic Hudson River region, the winery grows its own grapes and produces some vintage varietals. Among the French hybrid varietal wines are de Chaunac, Leon Millot, Aurore, Seyval Blanc and Maréchal Foch. Cagnasso wines are available only at the winery.

The tasting room at Cagnasso Winery is a very old barn surrounded by vineyards and orchards (ABOVE). The winery is in an adjacent modern building.

CASA LARGA VINEYARDS

Casa Larga Vineyards, located near Rochester in the Finger Lakes District, is the first farm winery in Monroe County. The vinifera vineyard was founded in 1974 and will eventually cover 40 acres of hilltop land. Winemaking was begun in 1978 and annual production is now around 5,000 gallons. All 11 Casa Larga wines are 100 percent varietal and all are estate-grown, estate-bottled and vintage-dated. Three white wines from Casa

Larga stand out: Gewürztraminer, Pinot Chardonnay and Johannisberg Riesling, all award-winners. Other whites are Aurora and Delaware. The red wines include Cabernet Sauvignon, Pinot Noir and de Chaunac.

CASCADE MOUNTAIN VINEYARDS

A small, family-farm winery on the eastern slopes of the Hudson Valley in Dutchess County, Cascade Mountain Vineyards produces 6,000 cases of wine annually. Most are sold in advance by subscription. The premium wines are Cascade Mountain White, made primarily from Aurora with a touch of Vignoles, Cascade Mountain Rosé, a well-received dry wine, and Reserved Red, a vintage-dated, Burgundian-style wine. Cascade Mountain also makes a rich, fresh New Harvest Red similar to a Beaujolais. The house wines are a good value and include Cascade Mountain Red, Le Hamburgér Red and A Little White Wine, which is light, fresh and dry.

BELOW *Grapes are hand-harvested on Flint Hill, part of Cascade Mountain Vineyards. These are used for premium wines.*

CHATEAU ESPERANZA WINERY

The Greek Revival stone mansion called Chateau Esperanza was completed in 1838. On a bluff above Keuka Lake in the Finger Lakes region, the house became the home of Chateau Esperanza Winery in 1979. The only winery in the east to be owned and operated entirely by women, it has been extremely successful in a short time, winning awards since the first vintage. Production at Chateau Esperanza is about 8,500 gallons a year, but will increase when the winery's six acres of vineyard begin to produce.

COTTAGE VINEYARDS

Owner/winemaker Allan MacKinnon concentrates his energies on producing solid, well-made Seyval Blanc and red table wine. Cottage Vineyards is located in the Hudson River region. The vineyard covers about four acres, and anticipated production is approaching 5,000 gallons a year. Very much a one-man operation, MacKinnon thinks his winery may be the smallest commercial one in the country.

DEMAY WINE CELLARS

Serge DeMay came to the Finger Lakes area from France planning only to grow grapes. His passion for winemaking took over, however, and the winery now produces a number of vintage-dated wines. The white wines from DeMay are Chablis Blanc, Delaware and a dry, grapey Niagara. The red wines are de Chaunac, Baco Noir and Landot, a delicate, light wine. DeMay also produces Brut and sweet sparkling wines, both naturally fermented in the bottle.

FOUR CHIMNEYS FARM WINERY

On the west shore of Seneca Lake in the Finger Lakes region, Four Chimneys is a small winery producing wines from organically grown grapes. No fertilizers or pesticides are used on the 15 acres of vineyard. Four Chimneys was founded in 1980, and now produces about 4,000 gallons of 16 different wines annually. These unusual wines have been rather successful — the Riesling and Catawba took silver medals at the 1981 New York State Fair.

GLENORA WINE CELLARS

On the shores of Seneca Lake in the historic Finger Lakes region, Glenora Wine Cellars is a highly successful enterprise founded in 1977. The grapes, both vinifera and French hybrid types, come from 250 acres of vineyard controlled by the winery. Annual production is around 20,000 cases. Glenora has recently ceased the production of red wines in order to concentrate on five varietal whites: Chardonnay, Johannisberg Riesling, Ravat Blanc, Cayuga and Seyval Blanc. Sparkling wine from Chardonnay grapes is also now being made at Glenora by the *méthode champenoise*; the first release is scheduled for 1984 and is eagerly awaited.

Glenora Wine Cellars wines have won a number of awards, in competition not only with other New York wines but also with California and European wines. The Johannisberg Riesling and Chardonnay have done particularly well.

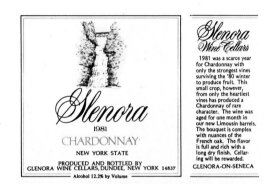

GREAT WESTERN WINERY

The Great Western Winery, near the village of Hammondsport in the Finger Lakes region, is one of the oldest producers of premium and champagne-style wines in America. The original winery was built in 1860 and was the first winery in the region. Today, Great Western labels still bear the designation Bonded Winery No.1. Under the name Pleasant Valley, the winery became famous for its sparkling wine. It survived Prohibition by selling sacramental and medicinal wines, and after Repeal, the winery steadily grew. In 1962, it was acquired by the Taylor Wine Company, its neighbor for 82 years; in 1977, Taylor in turn became part of The Coca-Cola Company. The Great Western Winery is currently the producer of a line of 26 premium New York State wines, including sparkling wines, varietals, table wines and Solera dessert wines and vermouths. Beginning in 1981, Great

BELOW *Several additions have been made since this building was erected in 1860. It housed the original cellars of the Great Western Winery. Courtesy of the Great Western Winery.*

Western introduced limited-edition, vintage-dated, 100 per cent New York State Special Selection wines. The first wines included Verdelet, Aurora Blanc, Rosé of de Chaunac and Vidal Ice Wine. The availability of the wines and varietals changes from year to year according to the quality of the vintage for each variety.

These are the Solera aging cellars of the Great Western Winery (ABOVE). The winery produce a large variety of wines including some excellent sherries.

HARGRAVE VINEYARD

The North Fork of Long Island is blessed with rich, well-drained soil and a temperate climate as a result of the moderating influence of Peconic Bay and Long Island Sound. Despite these advantages, Alex and Louisa Hargrave were nonetheless pioneers in growing wine grapes in this region when they planted their vineyard in 1973. Other vineyards and wineries have since been established on the North Fork, but Hargrave still stands out. Production is small and anticipated to rise only to 8,000 cases a year.

Hargrave produces several fine wines using French varietal grapes. Notable are the award-winning Chardonnays, including the 1981 "Collector's Series." Cabernet Sauvignon from Hargrave has been well received and the "Reserve" from 1978 is another award-winner.

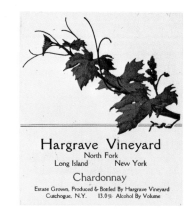

HERON HILL VINEYARDS

On Bully Hill above Lake Keuka in the Finger Lakes region, Heron Hill is a fairly new and small operation. Vinifera grapes are grown in a 30-acre vineyard and are used to produce about 8,000 cases a year of Chardonnay and Johannisberg Riesling. Both are estate-bottled and both are quite good.

Johnson Estate Wines

Grapes have been grown on the Johnson Estate for well over a century and the Johnson Winery, established in 1961, is the oldest exclusively estate winery in New York. Located on the southeastern shore of Lake Erie in Chatauqua County, the winery produces a number of award-winning wines. Blanc de Blancs Sec is crisp and very dry, similar to a Fumé Blanc; Chatauqua Blanc is a notable semi-dry white with a refreshing flavor; Delaware is a fruity, slightly musky semi-dry wine, and Liebeströpfchen ("Little Love Drops"), is rich, fruity and semi-sweet. Johnson Estate produces two red wines, the semi-sweet Ives Noir and the classic, dry Chancellor Noir.

Lenz Vineyards

Pat and Peter Lenz sold their four-star restaurant in 1977 and then spent a year traveling cross-country looking at possible vineyard locations. They decided on the North Fork of Long Island because of its climate, soil and proximity to New York City. The 30-acre vineyard is planted to a number of varietal grapes. The first wines from Lenz have just been released. Notable are Nouveau of Pinot Noir and Gewürztraminer. A chateau-style blend of Merlot, Cabernet Sauvignon and Cabernet Franc is planned.

McGregor Vineyard Winery

McGregor Vineyard Winery is a small, premium estate winery. The first major vinifera planting in the vineyard was in 1973 and the plantings now total 20 acres of six varieties. Varietal wines from McGregor include Chardonnay, Riesling, Gewürztraminer, Pinot Noir and Cayuga. Late Harvest Rieslings with very high sugar content are produced each year from botrytized grapes.

Needleman Winery

A very new, very small winery on Long Island's North Fork, Needleman Winery produces only one wine, a drinkable, light red table wine called Little Peconic Red. Winemaker Fletcher Weintraub, Jr. uses grapes from a selected number of New York growers to produce some 300 cases of this wine a year.

Northeast Vineyard

Northeast Vineyard is the smallest bonded winery in the country. Only 500 gallons a year are produced from the two-acre vineyard. The wines are made with indigenous yeast and no sulfur, and are aged in Kentucky oak for two years before release. Red wine from Foch grapes have won several prestigious medals in the past.

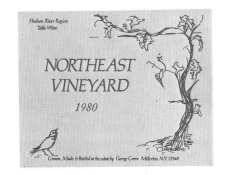

North Salem Vineyard

The only vineyard in Westchester County, North Salem Vineyard was founded by Dr. George Naumburg in 1965. After much experimentation, he settled on one white grape, Seyval Blanc and smaller amounts of several red grapes. Until 1980, North Salem sold grapes and juice to home winemakers; it became a winery in 1979 and opened for sales in 1981. Recent production from the 18 acres of vines has been under 1,000 cases a year, but new plantings should increase the production to about 3,500 cases of Seyval Blanc and smaller amounts of red wines.

PLANE'S CAYUGA VINEYARDS

Grapes from Mary and Bob Plane's vineyard on the west shore of Cayuga Lake in the Finger Lakes region have been in demand by premium wineries since 1975. In 1980, the Planes decided to open their own winery, and made 434 cases of three different wines. Since then, they have continued to produce a number of wines, with a production goal of 10,000 cases annually.

Three wines dominate the Plane selections because of their consistent high quality. The Chardonnay is buttery and rich, an equal match for the best California equivalent. Cayuga White is made from a grape developed expressly for the Finger Lakes region. It produces a delicate, dry wine. Of the 16 red grape varieties planted experimentally at the Plane vineyard, the first to show real promise was Chancellor. The wine is well-balanced and full-bodied.

ROTOLO & ROMEO WINES

Tom Rotolo and Paul Romeo established their winery in an old macaroni plant in 1980. Using grapes from the famed Naples area of the Finger Lakes region, they produce just one wine — de Chaunac. Annual production of this dry, light red wine is now about 2,000 gallons. Rotolo & Romeo de Chaunac is 100 percent varietal and every bottle is vintage-dated.

The Taylor Wine Company was a pioneer in the use of the mechanical harvester in the 1960s. One is at work here (RIGHT) *in the company's vineyards. Courtesy of The Taylor Wine Company, Inc.*

TAYLOR WINE COMPANY

Founded in 1880 on a seven-acre plot of vineyards overlooking Keuka Lake in the Finger Lakes region, the Taylor Wine Company has grown to become the largest producer of premium and champagne-style wines in the eastern United States. The company survived Prohibition by selling sacramental wine and grape juice; which was particularly popular. Taylor began making sparkling wine in the 1930s by the *méthode champenoise*; in 1968, the company switched to the transfer method of production. At present, there are over 12 million bottles aging at any given time. In 1961, Taylor Wine Company acquired its next-door neighbor, the Pleasant Valley Wine Company. In 1977, the company became a member of The Wine Spectrum, a wholly owned subsidiary of The Coca-Cola Company.

In addition to being the leading producer of premium sparkling and dessert wines in America, Taylor produces a range of table wines.

Taylor and Great Western New York State Champagnes are produced by the transfer process, which allows for fermentation and aging in the bottle. The mechanized, high-speed bottling line is shown in operation here (LEFT). *Courtesy of The Taylor Wine Company, Inc.*

VALLEY VINEYARDS

Valley Vineyards is a small, picturesque estate winery and vineyard located among the foothills of Ulster County's Shawangunk Mountains. Production is currently over 4,000 gallons a year — 10,000 gallons are expected by 1985. Five estate-bottled wines are available: Autumn White, Pinot Noir, Cayuga White, Seyval and Autumn Red.

WICKHAM VINEYARDS LTD.

For well over a century the Wickham Vineyards have produced fine grapes in the Finger Lakes region. The eastern slopes along Seneca Lake support 165 acres of grapes, mostly French hybrids. The winery, built in 1981, produces over 25,000 gallons each year, with the emphasis on premium white wines. Although Wickham is a new winery, it has already won several awards, particularly for its Aurora Dry, Aurora Semi-Dry and Cayuga White. The most notable of the other wines produced at Wickham include Chardonnay, Catawba and Delaware.

BELOW The new winery at Wickham Vineyards overlooks the vineyards and Seneca Lake. The winery boasts two large production cellars and a warehouse.

HERMANN J. WIEMER VINEYARD

From 1970 to 1980, Hermann Wiemer was head winemaker at Bully Hill Vineyards. In 1979, he founded his own vineyard in the same area, on Seneca Lake in the Finger Lakes region. His 50 acres of vineyard are planted mostly to Riesling and Chardonnay grapes; they yield about 2,500 cases a year. The emphasis is on excellent Rieslings, which are produced in the classic Mosel style of Mr. Wiemer's native Germany. The winery also produces highly regarded Pinot Chardonnay. All Wiemer wines are vintage-dated and estate-bottled.

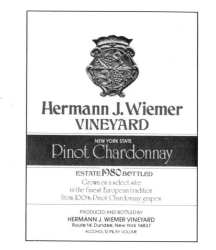

WINDSOR VINEYARDS

Some unusual offerings distinguish Windsor Vineyards which is located on the Hudson River in Southern Ulster County. For instance, each bottle is given a personalized label and premium California wines can be found in their tasting room or ordered through the mail. The winery produces a sparkling, champagne-style wine using the *méthode champenoise*. It also makes its own version of premium, vintage-dated French hybrid wines. These include, among others, Vincent Noir, Seyval Blanc and Aurora. All the wines are of consistently excellent quality.

BELOW *Wine-producing areas of New York State are situated in the north and to the east of New York City. The Finger Lakes region in the north first entered the winemaking field in the 1850s. It has a tough climate for vine-growing with very severe winters, but warm summers. The Hudson River and North Fork regions have less extreme growing conditions and good soil. These new areas are now producing excellent grapes.*

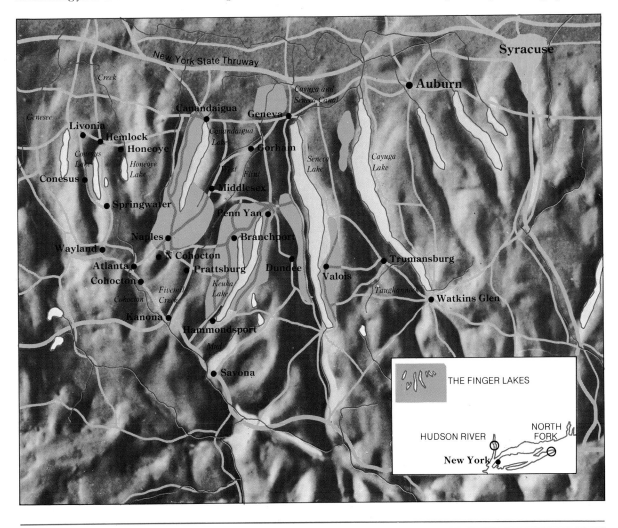

THE WINES OF THE
PACIFIC NORTHWEST

Winemaking in Washington, Oregon and Idaho has experienced a tremendous upsurge in the past decade. These states have always been known as superior fruit- and berry-producing regions, and they lie in the same latitudes as Burgundy and Bordeaux. It is only reasonable that growers in these states would adapt to the increasing interest in wine throughout America.

WASHINGTON

The Cascade Mountains of Washington serve as a rain barrier, making the west side of the state on Puget Sound cool and wet, and the interior Columbia, Snake River and Yakima Valleys dry and warm. As a result, most of the wine-growing in the state is concentrated in that area of south-central Washington. Among the wineries are Chateau Ste. Michelle, Preston Wine Cellars and Yakima River Winery.

OREGON

Most of the vineyards in Oregon are new and small, but very promising. Many lie in the Willamette Valley to the south and west of Portland in western Oregon. Some are found in the Umpqua Valley in the southwestern part of the state, near Eugene, and some are even further south near Roseburg.

Washington and Yamhill Counties Washington County is due west of Portland, on a straight line to the Pacific. The county holds half a dozen wineries, including Côte des Colombes, Tualatin and Elk Cove. Yamhill County is to the southwest of Portland, bordering on Washington County. It too is crowded with well-known wineries, including Knudsen Erath, Sokol Blosser, Chateau Benoit and Amity Vineyards. Other vineyards in the area include Serendipity Cellars and Nehalem Bay Wine Company.

Eugene Some of the better known wineries found in the Eugene area are Forgeron, Alpine and Hinman.

Douglas County Near Roseburg in Douglas County is the Henry Winery; further south, near the California border, is Siskiyou Vineyards.

IDAHO

The small vineyards of Idaho lie in the area between the state capital, Boise, and the Snake River, in the western part of the state. The first winery in Idaho, Ste. Chapelle, was established in 1976. The volcanic ash in the area provides good drainage and the climate is sunny with cool nights. Facelli Vineyards opened there in 1979.

WASHINGTON

CHATEAU STE. MICHELLE

Chateau Ste. Michelle is Washington's foremost producer of premium table wines. Starting with the first harvest year in 1967, the winery has pioneered the planting of vinifera grapes in its vineyards in the Columbia Valley, east of the Cascade Mountains. This area, near the confluence of the Columbia, Yakima and Snake Rivers, is similar to the Bordeaux and Burgundy regions of France. The first harvest at Chateau Ste. Michelle produced 6,000 cases; current production is 250,000 cases a year, with 500,000 cases projected for the future.

The number of varietal wines made by Chateau Ste. Michelle has increased over the years. The white wines now include Johannisberg Riesling, Chenin Blanc, Fumé Blanc, Semillon Blanc, Gewürztraminer, Muscat Canelli and Chardonnay. Grenache Rosé and Rosé of Cabernet, Merlot, Cabernet and Cabernet Sauvignon complete the list. Each of the wines has been a consistent award-winner at national and international competitions. When conditions are right, a botrytized late-harvest Johannisberg Riesling and a rare Ice Wine White Riesling are made. A dry *méthode champenoise* sparkling wine made from Pinot Noir grapes is also produced.

BELOW *The manor house at Chateau Ste. Michelle is on an 87-acre wooded estate, with gardens designed by the same Olmstead brothers who designed New York's Central Park. The winery is behind the manor.*

HINZERLING VINEYARDS

Hinzerling Vineyards is a limited-production winery operated by the Wallace family. Their 25-acre vineyard on the north side of the Yakima Valley was planted in 1972; the first crush was in 1976. About 15,000 gallons are now made at the winery. Some 80 percent of the production is in white wine. Hinzerling specializes in making late- and special-harvest wines from botrytized White Riesling and Gewürztraminer grapes. In addition, dry and off-dry White Rieslings and Gewürztraminers are made, as well as full-bodied Chardonnays, Cabernet Sauvignons and Merlots.

BELOW *Barrels of experimental wines age in the Hinzerling Vineyards cellar. The winery is experimenting with the traditional bottle-fermentation of sparkling wines.*

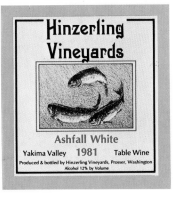

LOST MOUNTAIN WINERY

Very new and very small, operations at Lost Mountain Winery began in September 1981. In 1982, production was doubled to reach 650 gallons. Owner Romeo J. Conca has no plans to raise production above 1,000 gallons a year. The winery specializes in red wines produced from grapes grown in eastern Washington and California. It is still far too soon to judge their quality.

PRESTON WINE CELLARS

The southern Columbia River Basin area of Washington state is one of the newer and most promising wine-growing regions of the Pacific Northwest. Preston Wine Cellars, Washington's largest family-owned winery, is located here, with 181 acres of 10 vinifera varietal grapes. The vineyards were planted from 1972 to 1979; the winery was built in 1976. About 150,000 gallons of a number of different wines are produced each year. Many of the wines are award-winning successes, particularly outstanding are the Chardonnay, Fumé Blanc and Chenin Blanc.

TUCKER CELLARS

The first crush at Tucker Cellars, a small, family-owned winery, was in 1981. The result in 1982 was three well-received wines, a very dry Johannisberg Riesling, a dry White Riesling and a semi-dry Chenin Blanc. The winery has 30 acres of

Gewürztraminer grapes at Hinzerling Vineyards are picked by hand. Those shown here are botrytized; they are laid out in trays ready for production. As the first step the wine press is filled with grapes (INSET).

varietal grapes under cultivation, but these will not be in full production for several years. In the meantime, grapes are purchased from local growers in the Yakima Valley. Annual production at Tucker Cellars has been rising steadily to 24,000 gallons a year. New varieties, including Cabernet Sauvignon, Chardonnay and Gewürztraminer, have been added. There are plans for the future to include special bottlings of the late-harvest and ice wines.

MANFRED VIERTHALER WINERY

The Puyallup and Carbon River Valleys of western Washington are well-suited for growing German vinifera grapes. The Manfred Vierthaler Winery, which began production in 1976, specializes in German-style wines, particularly Rieslings.

WORDEN'S WASHINGTON WINERY

Worden's Washington Winery made a promising start with its 1980 Johannisberg Riesling, which won numerous gold medals in competition with other Northwest wines. The winery buys all its grapes from Washington growers. With a capacity of 20,000 gallons, it is the fifth largest in the state. Owner Jack Worden plans to expand to 50,000 gallons over the next few years. In addition to its famed Johannisberg Rieslings, Worden's also produces Fumé Blanc, Chardonnay, Gamay Beaujolais Rosé, Traminer (Gewürztraminer) and Late Harvest Gewürztraminer.

YAKIMA RIVER WINERY

A limited-production winery located in the center of the Yakima Valley, the Yakima River Winery is owned by the Rauner family. It produces 4,000 cases a year of vintage-dated varietal wines, using grapes from selected vineyards in the valley. The first vintage was in 1979. The winery produces several award-winning wines, including a highly regarded Johannisberg Riesling. Other wines are Chardonnay, Chenin Blanc, Gewürztraminer, Cabernet Sauvignon and Merlot. Valley Rosé using Catawba grapes is also made.

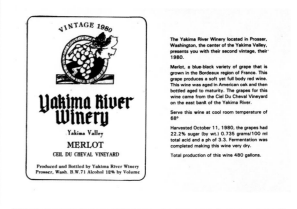

OREGON

ALPINE VINEYARDS

The first plantings in the 20-acre Alpine Vineyards were established in 1976. In the foothills of the Coast Range Mountains, the winery is 30 miles northwest of Eugene. It opened in 1980, offering only estate-bottled wines. Alpine wines are available only in limited quantities and they have

148

been critically praised. The 1981 White Riesling has won a number of medals. Pinot Noir and Chardonnay from Alpine are generally of high quality; Cabernet Sauvignon and Gewürztraminer, which are soon to be released for the first time, should be of an equally high standard.

AMITY VINEYARDS

Amity Vineyards is located in western Oregon on 70 hilly acres, 45 miles from Portland. The site, with a small existing vineyard, was purchased in 1974; the winery was built in 1976 and operations expanded in 1977. About half the production at Amity is from estate-grown grapes; the remainder is from grapes grown in the Pacific Northwest. A good range of wines is made at the winery, including Rieslings in the dry Alsatian style and a Beaujolais-style Pinot Noir Nouveau. Amity Chardonnay has been a medal-winner but the winery is probably most famous for its excellent Pinot Noir. In an extensive tasting of American Pinot Noirs held by *Vintage* magazine in 1981, the 1978 Oregon Pinot Noir from Amity was hailed as being of outstanding quality.

CHATEAU BENOIT

In 1972, Dr. Fred Benoit planted 10 acres of grapes near Veneta, west of Eugene, for recreation. The hobby became obsessive. In 1979, Benoit decided to devote all his time to the vineyard, and moved the operation to Lafayette, where a new winery is under construction. Located in the northern Willamette Valley, the new winery is now producing about 20,000 gallons a year. The style at Chateau Benoit is light and European. The Rieslings from Oregon and Washington grapes have been well received, as have the Sauvignon Blancs. The first Cabernet Sauvignon was made in the fall of 1982 and has not yet been released. Sparkling wines are another new development at Chateau Benoit, and one that the owners hope to place more emphasis on in the future. The first *cuvée* of Pinot Noir and Chardonnay grapes has not yet been released.

COTE DES COLOMBES VINEYARD

A small vineyard founded in 1977, Côte des Colombes is in the northern Willamette Valley. The 10 acres of vineyard are planted primarily to Pinot Noir, Cabernet Sauvignon and Gamay, and it is for these wines that the winery is known. The Cabernets and Gamays have won a number of regional awards. Chenin Blanc is also made from grapes grown in Washington. The winery produces about 10,000 gallons a year. An interesting experiment at Côte des Colombes is the use of Oregon white oak to make the barrels used for aging Pinot Noir. The barrels now hold the 1982 pressing, which is due to be released in 1985, but it is possible that it may be held back for further aging, depending on the success of its results.

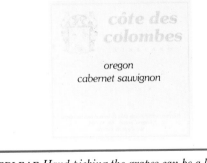

OVERLEAF *Hand-picking the grapes can be a long and arduous business, but many vineyards still harvest in this way. It ensures that the vines are treated with care.*

ELK COVE VINEYARDS

In the foothills of the Oregon Coast Range, above the Willamette Valley, Elk Cove Vineyards was established by Pat and Joe Campbell in 1974. The vineyard has grown to 22 acres, with an additional 30 acres planned in the next few years. The vineyard now provides about 70 percent of the winery's needs; grapes are also purchased from nearby growers. In regional competitions, Elk Cove wines have been standouts. Intense spicy aromas and full, complex flavors characterize Elk Cove Pinot Noirs; the Chardonnays are richly varietal wines that have sufficient fruit and acidity to age well. Several styles of Riesling are produced each year, but all are distinguished by fresh, floral aromas and intense varietal fruit. In addition, small quantities of Cabernet Sauvignon and Gewürztraminer are being made, but it is too soon to tell if the Willamette Valley is really the right place for these grapes.

THE EYRIE VINEYARDS

In 1966, David and Diana Lett began the planting of their 20-acre vineyard in the Red Hills of Dundee. It was the first planting of premium wine grapes in the Willamette Valley in 50 years, and it made the Letts legendary figures in Oregon wine history. David Lett was convinced that the cool climate was perfect for Pinot Noir and Chardonnay — and he was absolutely right. Eyrie Vineyards wines have won many regional and international awards, including an "Outstanding Quality" ranking from *Vintage* magazine for the 1976 Pinot Noir. Production at the winery, located in McMinnville, eight miles from the vineyard, is deliberately limited to 10,000 gallons

annually, primarily of subtle, delicate Pinot Noir and crisp, refined Chardonnay. Smaller amounts of Pinot Gris and Muscat Ottonel, which are two varieties that the Letts pioneered in the United States, are also made at the winery and are of a particularly high standard.

FORGERON VINEYARD

The Forgeron Vineyard exploded onto the Oregon wine scene with its first crush in 1978, when it produced an outstanding White Riesling that is now a collector's item. Located in Lane County in the Willamette Valley, the winery has 20 acres under cultivation, with 12 in actual production. Owner Lee Smith plans to expand to 40 to 45 acres, and produce about 25,000 gallons a year but, currently, production is fairly low. Although Forgeron first achieved fame with its Riesling, it is Pinot Noir that has maintained the winery's reputation for excellence.

HENRY WINERY

When Scott Henry first planted grapes on 12 acres of his family's ranch in the Umpqua Valley, the neighbors were amazed. That was in 1972, and since then the vineyard has been expanded to 28 acres. A winery was built in 1978. The southern Oregon climate has proved ideal for Chardonnay, Pinot Noir and Gewürztraminer, and Henry Estate wines from these grapes have done consistently well in competition throughout the Pacific Northwest. All Henry Estate wines, including the red table wine, are estate-grown and estate-bottled.

HINMAN VINEYARDS

A new addition to the growing wine industry in Oregon, Hinman Vineyards was founded in 1979. Using grapes from a 10-acre vineyard established by Doyle Hinman in 1972, the first crush yielded

BELOW *The winery at Hinman Vineyards is built into the hillside to help maintain cool temperatures.*

330 cases. Later crushes have increased the production, helped by grapes from an additional nine-acre vineyard planted in 1980. In the future, production at the winery will increase to 9,000 cases a year. Hinman Vineyards has been praised at several Northwest wine judgings. The wines available, all vintage-dated and estate-bottled, include Riesling, Gewürztraminer, White Cabernet, Chardonnay, White Pinot Noir, Pinot Noir and Cabernet Sauvignon.

KNUDSEN ERATH WINERY

One of the older wineries in Oregon, Knudsen Erath Winery was founded in 1969. The winery now has nearly 100 acres of vines planted in the Chehalem foothills of the northern Willamette Valley, with an additional 30 planned for the near future. Production is now over 13,000 cases a year, making Knudsen Erath the largest producer of strictly Oregon wines. The winery has established a critical reputation for its dry White Rieslings and French-style Pinot Noir. Both have won a number of awards, and are quite reasonably priced. Chardonnay from Knudsen Erath is also excellent; it is well-balanced, fruity and properly buttery. Sparkling wine, fast becoming an Oregon specialty, is now being made at the winery; the first release of 1,000 cases was in the fall of 1983.

NEHALEM BAY WINE COMPANY

Nehalem Bay Wine Company originally opened in 1973 as a fruit and berry winery, but in 1976 it began to make the vinifera wines that are now its main product. It is the only winery on the Oregon coast, and for that reason it has to buy its grapes from Northwest growers in the Yakima Valley of Washington and the Willamette Valley of Oregon. Owner Patrick McCoy has planted a five-acre vineyard that he hopes will bear fruit by 1986, despite its less than ideal location. The winery occupies a former cheese factory and has a storage capacity of 20,000 gallons.

OAK KNOLL WINERY

Since its founding in 1970, Oak Knoll has grown steadily to become one of Oregon's biggest wineries. Annual production is now about 50,000 gallons a year, mostly in high-quality fruit and berry wines. A small but growing amount of well-received varietal grape wines is also produced. Oak Knoll buys almost all its fruit from other

growers in the area. Some of the grapes come from Washington state, but most come from the nearby Dion Vineyards. In total, there are 16 wines available from Oak Knoll, although this includes rhubarb, blackberry, red currant, gooseberry and plum varieties. Among the grape wines are Pinot Noir Blanc, White Riesling, Pinot Noir Rosé, Muscat of Alexandria, Chardonnay, Washington Cabernet Sauvignon, Pinot Noir, Gewürztraminer and Niagara.

PONZI VINEYARDS

One of the pioneer wineries in the northern Willamette Valley, Ponzi Vineyards is near the Tualatin River, 15 miles south of Portland. The 11½-acre vineyard was planted in 1970. Besides their own grapes, the Ponzi family uses grapes grown within a 10-mile radius to produce nearly 12,000 gallons of wine each year. Among Oregon wine-drinkers, Ponzi White Riesling is highly respected. Dry and slightly tart, it is also quite reasonably priced. The Pinot Noir and Chardonnay are two other wines that stand out from the rest. An unusual variety known as Pinot Gris is now in production at the winery. Although *gris* means grey, and although the mature grapes are almost maroon, this is a white wine with a rather heavy yet fresh flavor.

SERENDIPITY CELLARS WINERY

The owners of Serendipity Cellars Winery, Glen and Cheryl Longshore, describe their operation as a "miniscule boutique winery". It is an accurate summation: production in the winery's first year was 1,500 gallons, with 7,500 projected as the final goal. Serendipity uses grapes from growers in Polk County and the Willamette Valley region

of western Oregon. In additon to Chardonnay and Chenin Blanc, the winery produces Pinot Noir Rosé, Pinot Noir Blanc and Pinot Noir Fruité. The Fruité is a Beaujolais-style red with the emphasis on fruity flavor; the Longshores feel it will become one of their specialties.

SHAFER VINEYARD CELLARS

Before opening their winery in 1981, Harvey and Linda Shafer sold grapes commercially from their 20-acre vineyard, planted in 1972. Nestled in the foothills of the Willamette Valley in the Gales Creek area west of Portland, the winery produced 3,500 gallons in its first year of operation; its maximum capacity is 15,000 gallons. Shafer has received numerous awards, including a gold medal for its 1979 Pinot Noir. Other excellent Shafer wines include Chardonnay and Riesling, and a new wine, Pinot Noir Blanc.

SISKIYOU VINEYARDS

Only 20 miles from the California border, Siskiyou Vineyards is Oregon's southernmost winery. The first plantings in the 12-acre vineyard in the Rogue River Basin were begun in 1974; the 15,000-gallon winery was bonded in

These fermenting vats (ABOVE) at Sokol Blosser Winery are used for the production of white wines. In the background is initial fermentation of red wine must. This process is fairly rapid and produces a lot of carbon dioxide.

THE WINES OF
OTHER STATES

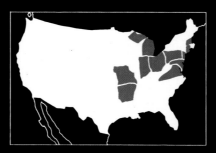

With the possible exception of Alaska, virtually every state in America does or could make wine. There is a winery making pineapple wine in Hawaii, and two in Florida make orange wine. We have confined this book chiefly to serious wineries making grape wine, however, and even that has occasionally threatened to get out of hand! Below is a brief description of some of the less well-known wine-producing states. Much of the wine is available only at the wineries and much of it has therefore been undeservedly neglected. You may be pleasantly surprised by the excellent local wines.

Arkansas Parts of the state resemble the lower Swiss Alps. The Swiss immigrants who settled there began an ongoing tradition of light Swiss-style wines.

Connecticut A new region, with characteristics similar to those of the Hudson River region of New York State.

Indiana It is far too soon to tell, but French hybrid grapes should do well.

Maryland Boordy Vineyards near the Pontomac River pioneered in introducing French hybrids to the United States.

Massachusetts The state encourages viticulture, the home of Commonwealth Winery.

Michigan Small but growing premium wine industry. The climate of the Leelanau Peninsula in the north of the state is fairly good for grapes, but the winters are cold.

Missouri At one time, Missouri was the second-largest wine-producing state in the country. Prohibition virtually destroyed the industry, but it is now making a strong comeback, with help from the state government. This is an area to watch.

New Jersey The terrain and climate have potential, but it will be a while before serious judgements can be made.

Ohio Historically, Ohio was important to the early growth of American winemaking, but the area is now relatively unimportant. The potential for a serious comeback is there. The Hafle Vineyards have opened here.

Pennsylvania Another rapidly growing area, again encouraged by the state government. It has good potential. Among the vineyards are the Kollu, Lembo, Stephen Bahn and Mount Hope Wineries.

Virginia Thomas Jefferson grew grapes and made wine at Monticello and the tradition continues. The vineyards in Virginia began to take off in the early 1970s with the introduction of suitable new hybrid vines. The climate is excellent for wine-growing and the terrain is suitably hilly. Virginia may be causing a lot of excitement in wine circles in a few years from now.

ARKANSAS

WIEDERKEHR WINE CELLARS

When he settled in the foothills of the Ozarks in the Arkansas River Valley, the area reminded Johann Wiederkehr of his native Swiss Alps. He planted his first vines in 1880 and built a wine cellar that still stands. Wiederkehr Wine Cellars is run by Johann's grandsons, and is the oldest winery in the southeast.The vineyards have expanded to cover nearly 600 acres and annual production is about 400,000 cases of award-winning wines.

Wiederkehr produces a full line of varietal wines. Of particular interest is the Arkansas Mountain Cynthiana. This is a fragrant, heavy-bodied dry red varietal wine made from grapes native to Arkansas. Also interesting is Di Tanta Maria, a blend of three muscat grape varieties. It is a pale golden color with a soft, sweet quality. Verdelet Blanc is a dry, delicate white table wine, with a crisp, slightly flinty taste.

CONNECTICUT

HAMLET HILL VINEYARDS

Reasoning that since wild grapes grew well on Hamlet Hill in northeastern Connecticut, cultivated varieties would too, Gus Loos planted his first five acres of vines in 1975. Half the original planting was in Seyve-Villard #5276, a French hybrid white grape that is the source of Seyval Blanc. The other half was in a variety of French hybrid reds. The first harvest was in 1978, and the results were encouraging enough to justify planting an additional nine acres. A winery was built after the 1979 vintage. Dr. Howard Bursen, formerly of Bully Hill Vineyards, is the winemaker there.

Hamlet Hill produces a 100-percent varietal Riesling that is medium-dry with an intense flowery aroma. The Seyval Blanc is estate-bottled, and is dry and crisp. Of the blended wines, White Reel is a medium-dry white, Drumlin Rose is a light, medium-dry rosé and Charter Oak Red is estate-bottled and aged for more than 18 months in oak barrels.

HOPKINS VINEYARD

Hopkins Vineyard is a new venture located on Lake Waramaug in the northwestern corner of Connecticut. The vineyard is planted to 20 acres of French-American hybrids; the winery was built in a renovated barn in 1980.

At present Hopkins Vineyard makes four wines. Barn Red is a light red wine made from Maréchal Foch grapes. Waramaug White is a crisp white wine made from Aurora grapes; the Sachem's Picnic red wine is made from the Leon Millet grape and Seyval Blanc is a fruity white wine made from high-quality, hand-picked grapes. Although young,this vineyard is already showing considerable promise.

STONECROP VINEYARDS

The first vines at Stonecrop Vineyards were planted in 1977, on the historic homestead of Paul Wheeler. The first harvest was in 1979. In addition to French hybrids, Stonecrop grows a small amount of Cabernet Sauvignon and Chardonnay.

Stonecrop produces three varietal wines: a fruity, well-balanced Vidal Blanc, a crisp, clean Seyval Blanc and a 1980 estate-bottled Maréchal Foch. The Foch is fresh and dry, and receives no oak aging. An unvintaged Foch is also made. The 1980 estate-bottled White Table Wine is made from Rayon d'Or grapes. It has a flowery spiciness and is a good aperitif wine.

INDIANA

OLIVER WINE COMPANY

The Oliver Winery and Vineyards are pioneers in introducing French hybrid grapes and wines from those grapes to Indiana. The winery produces two generic red wines, Cellar Red Wine and Oliver Soft Red and a varietal Seyval Blanc. Oliver is well known in Indiana for its Camelot Mead, a light honey wine that is, so the winery claims, the most popular wine in Indiana.

MARYLAND

BOORDY VINEYARDS

Founded in 1945, Boordy Vineyards has established a solid reputation for carefully produced wines at reasonable prices. In 1980 Boordy passed into the hands of the R.B. Deford family. The winery is now located in Hydes, Maryland, in northeastern Baltimore County. Adjacent to the winery are 12 acres of vineyard, which do not provide enough fruit for the winery needs so that additional grapes are purchased from six major Maryland producers. Current production capacity is 16,000 gallons.

Boordy's standard wines are Maryland Red, Maryland White and Maryland Rosé. The specialty wines include Cedar Point Red, made entirely from grapes grown by the Cedar Point Vineyard, a varietal Seyval Blanc and a new red blend called Boordy Reserve. In addition, Boordy produces a Beaujolais-like red wine labeled as "Nouveau". Bottled each year on 15 November, this wine is fresh, slightly fruity and best enjoyed within its first year.

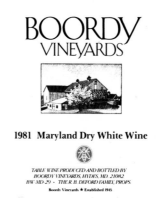

MONTBRAY WINE CELLARS

Set among the gentle hills of the Silver Run Valley, Montbray Wine Cellars became Maryland's third bonded winery in 1966. In that same year, Montbray became the first American winery to produce a varietally labeled wine from the French hybrid grape Seyve-Villard, otherwise known as Seyval Blanc. Each year 2,000 cases of Montbray wines are sold to the public.

Small quantities of varietal wines are made at

Montbray, including Pinot Chardonnay, Cabernet Sauvignon and Johannisberg Riesling. The winery is best known, however, for Seyval Blanc, Montbray Rosé and Montbray Red, a light, fruity wine with intriguing spiciness.

MONTBRAY
Maryland Chardonnay
WHITE TABLE WINE

ALCOHOL BY VOL. 12%
PRODUCED AND BOTTLED BY MONTBRAY WINE CELLARS LTD.
SILVER RUN VALLEY, WESTMINSTER, MD

ZIEM VINEYARDS

Ziem Vineyards is a very small winery located in Washington County, Maryland. The first vines were planted on the Ziem farm in 1972 on a five-acre plot. The winery was bonded in 1977. Present production is limited, aiming at modest growth each year. All Ziem Vineyards wines are dry, and almost all are 100 percent varietal. The red wines are unfiltered and unfined.

Ziem wines are eastern United States wines. The winery uses varietal French hybrid and native American grapes from its own vineyard and nearby vineyards in Maryland and Pennsylvania. Among the red wines are Chancellor, Chelois and Maréchal Foch; among the whites are Seyval Blanc, Dutchess and Vidal Blanc.

MASSACHUSETTS

COMMONWEALTH WINERY

Commonwealth Winery was the first winery in Massachusetts established under the 1978 Farm-Winery Act. Under the guidance of winemaker David Tower, the winery now produces over 12,000 cases of premium wines each year. It is ideally placed as it is within an hour's drive of downtown Boston.

Most Commonwealth wines are made from

French hybrid grapes. An exception is the tart Cranberry Apple Rosé. Among the white wines are the award-winning Seyval Blanc and Vidal Blanc, and also Aurora and Cayaga. The red wines include Foch and de Chaunac.

MICHIGAN

BOSKYDEL VINEYARD

On Lake Leelanau in northern Michigan, Boskydel Vineyard produces extremely high-quality wines made from French hybrid grapes. The 25 acres of vineyards are the result of years of experimentation, which were carried out in order to find the variety best suited to the area's climate, which is similar to that of northern

France. Production at Boskydel is limited but approaching 10,000 gallons a year.

Among the white wines from Boskydel are Vignoles, a crisp fruity wine resembling Chablis, Seyval Blanc and Johannisberg Riesling. The de Chaunac is ruby-red and rich. This grape is also used for a rosé.

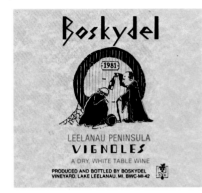

The concrete winery at Boskydel Vineyards (BELOW) overlooks Michigan's Lake Leelanau. It is built almost entirely underground to keep the wines cool as they age. The first snow in Michigan falls in October. LEFT *This young vineyard is under the first snowfall. Twenty-five acres of vines cover the hillsides of Boskydel. The first were planted in 1965.*

Part of Boskydel Vineyards overlooks the Lake Leelanau (BELOW), *where the climate can be extreme and grapes covered with snow* (BOTTOM). *Care of the vines is taken from the start by putting in trellising posts* (RIGHT).

L. MAWBY VINEYARDS/WINERY

A small, fairly new operation in northern Michigan on the Leelanau Peninsula, L. Mawby Vineyards consists of about nine acres of French hybrid varieties. Production is very small — the winery's goal is 500 cases a year.

Recent releases from L. Mawby are a 1980 Vignoles and a 1981 white table wine, which is made from a blend of Vignoles and Seyval Blanc grapes. The 1980 red table wine is made from Maréchal Foch grapes.

TABOR HILL VINEYARD AND WINECELLAR

The first hybrid grapes were planted at Tabor Hill in 1968. The light, sandy soil of Berrien County proved ideal for Baco Noir and Vidal Blanc, among others, and Tabor Hill's first vintage year was in 1971. Since then, the Bacos, Seyvals and Rieslings have been consistent award-winners.

The winery at Tabor Hill Vineyard (ABOVE) is near the shores of Lake Michigan, 90 miles from Chicago. The soil in the area seems to be especially good for Vidal grapes; this may become the true "Michigan varietal."

In addition to its hybrid wines, Tabor Hill produces several blends and some varietals. Cabernet Sauvignon and Pinot Chardonnay are made from out-of-state grapes; although the Berrien County Chardonnay is made from grapes which are grown at Tabor Hill.

MISSOURI

BIAS VINEYARDS AND WINERY

Jim and Norma Bias found a small Catawba vineyard on the farm they purchased in 1978. The vines had been planted in 1968. The new owners began making wine from their grapes in 1980 and have expanded the vineyards to include de Chaunac, Vidal and Seyval grapes.

Bias Vineyards produces three different wines from the Catawba grapes: Pink Catawba, Rosé and Dry Catawba. All are estate-bottled. The first wines from the French hybrid vines are due to be released in 1984.

MOUNT PLEASANT VINEYARDS

Before Prohibition, Missouri was the second-largest wine-producing state. Most of the state wineries, including Mount Pleasant, were located in the Augusta Valley of the Missouri River. Until 1920, Mount Pleasant wines were sold coast to coast. Since 1968, Mount Pleasant has again begun the production of a full line of wines from French hybrid grapes.

In total, Mount Pleasant produces 17 different wines, two of which are of exceptional interest. The first is Münch, a light, dry, red wine, which is produced from hybrid grapes developed by Thomas V. Munson, who was a famous nineteenth-century grape breeder. The second is a dessert wine, Stark's Star, which is the first of its type to be made in Missouri. This full-bodied red wine is made from a hybrid grape long thought to be extinct, but rediscovered in Missouri in 1978.

Stark's Star

A NATURAL DESSERT WINE
ALCOHOL 16% BY VOLUME
PRODUCED AND BOTTLED BY MOUNT PLEASANT VINEYARDS
AUGUSTA, MISSOURI

REIS WINERY

The vineyards at Reis Winery are located on the Missouri Ozark Plateau, at an elevation of 1,350 feet. More than 30 varieties of French hybrid and native American grapes are grown. Reis Winery wines fall into three categories: sweet native American, French hybrid blended and limited production. The limited production wines are made from French hybrid varietals and include a dry red Leon Millet, dry Seyval Blanc and Villard Blanc and a semi-dry white Vidal.

THE WINERY OF THE ABBEY

Southwest of St. Louis, the Winery of the Abbey produces a variety of wines from grapes grown in nearby vineyards in the Augusta region. The winery produces several wines, including Concord and White Concord. Its Missouri Riesling reflects the long tradition of German-style winemaking in Missouri.

NEW JERSEY

TEWKSBURY WINE CELLARS

The rolling hills of Hunterdon County in New Jersey are well-suited to the production of fine wines. Tewksbury Wine Cellars, founded in 1979, was the first premium winery in the area. This small operation produces about 10,000 gallons of wine a year, using chiefly grapes grown on 20 acres of vineyard.

Tewksbury concentrates on dry white wines. The vineyard is planted mostly to Chardonnay, Gewürztraminer and Riesling, although Tewksbury also produces Chenin Blanc, Seyval Blanc, Vilard Blanc and Cayuga White. The Vidal Blanc won a silver medal in a recent Eastern States Wine Competition.

OHIO

HAFLE VINEYARDS

BELOW *Owner Dan Haffle is testing the color and clarity of the end product by holding it up to the light. The look of the wine is an indication as to its quality.*

MAIN PICTURE *This is the common procedure of grafting two different grape varieties.* ABOVE *Sulfur dioxide is used to kill wild yeasts growing on the skins.*

Located just northwest of Springfield in Clark County, to the west of the Mad River, Hafle Vineyards grows premium French hybrid grapes. Owner Dan Hafle produces blended and varietal wines in a 60-year-old barn converted to a winery, and constantly seeks new grape varieties suitable for the Ohio climate. Among the wines produced at Hafle are Baco Noir, de Chaunac, Haut Sauterne and Concord, as well as a red table wine made from Chelois grapes and a white made from Villard Blanc.

PENNSYLVANIA

ALLEGRO VINEYARDS

The Brogue area of York County has permeable soil and a good climate for grapes. The Allegro Vineyards were established there between 1973 and 1978, growing about one-third vinifera and two-thirds hybrid. The first commercial vintage was in 1980. Production now is about 3,000 gallons, with 15,000 gallons the projected goal. In addition to Vin Blanc, Vin Rosé and Vin Rouge, Allegro produces three varietals, Seyval Blanc, Chardonnay and Cabernet Sauvignon. The winery has already won gold medals for its Cabernet and several awards for its other wines.

Allegro Vineyards raises a number of grape varieties, including Chardonnay, Petite Sirah, and Cabernet Sauvignon shown here (BELOW). *Partners Tim and John Crouch sell their wines throughout Pennsylvania, at the winery, and in selected stores in Washington, D.C.*

STEPHEN BAHN WINERY

A very small but growing winery, Stephen Bahn is located near the Susquehanna River in York County. The original vineyard was established in 1978, with expansions in 1980 and 1981. It now consists of four acres, planted to Pinot Noir, Chardonnay, Johannisberg Riesling and Gewürztraminer. Additional grapes are purchased from southern Pennsylvania growers. Production at the winery was only 175 cases in 1982, but more is anticipated in future vintages. This is a winery worth watching.

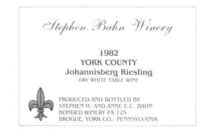

KOLLN VINEYARDS AND WINERY

Planting at Kolln Vineyards in Centre County began in 1971 with several hundred Delaware vines. Other varieties were added until 1975, when the vineyard reached its present size of 3,000 vines covering more than four acres. The winery operation began with the 1978 harvest and a production of 2,400 gallons. Recent harvests have been about 10 tons, which, together with additional grapes from Erie and Lancaster Counties, produce about 4,000 gallons of wine. Kolln Table Wines are blends of French hybrid and American grapes: Delaware and Aurora for the white wines; Steuben and Rosette for rosés; and de Chaunac, Foch and Baco Noir for reds. The dry white wine from Kolln won a silver medal at the 1982 Wineries Unlimited competition. It is a good, dry, fruity wine.

LAPIC WINERY

The only winery in Beaver County and the first limited winery in southwestern Pennsylvania, Lapic Winery is a family-owned and operated business. The vineyard was planted in 1968; three other growers now provide grapes as well. The winery was begun in 1977, with the production of 1,700 gallons. More than 10,000 gallons of 12 wines are now made each year, using French hybrid and American grapes.

LEMBO VINEYARDS AND WINERY

The Lembo family planted three varieties of French hybrid grapes in 1972 on the slopes of the Kishacoquillas Valley. After four years of care based on 70 years of family winemaking experience in Italy, the first grapes were harvested. In 1976, the Lembos established the first commercial winery in Mifflin County. Among the wines produced are Chelois, de Chaunac, Seyval Blanc, Chateau Antoinette, a semi-dry white, Lembruschini, a semi-dry red and Rosé.

The sandstone mansion at Mount Hope Winery (OVERLEAF) boasts 32 rooms and such details as hand-painted 18-foot ceilings. The estate gardens contain plants from all over the world.

MOUNT HOPE ESTATE & WINERY

The mansion on the Mount Hope estate was built in 1800. By 1900 its 32 rooms had been decorated in the height of Victorian fashion and they remain so today. Winemaking at Mount Hope began in 1979 with 10 acres of French hybrid wines. Annual production is now 50,000 gallons of a number of wines, including fruit wines. The Seyval Blanc and Vidal Blanc have both won gold medals.

BELOW *The banquet hall at Mount Hope mansion is filled with antiques recalling a bygone style of living. The property is listed in the National Register of Historic Places and was owned by the Grubb family until 1936.*

YORK SPRINGS VINEYARD AND WINERY

The vines at York Springs grow on the eastern slopes of the Appalachian Mountains in the Piedmont area. The winery produces Chardonnay and Seyval Blanc from varietal grapes. Red and rosé wines are made from an Alsatian hybrid. The white wines from York Springs are crisp, dry, and fruity; the red and rosé wines are also fruity, in the style of Beaujolais and Anjou.

VIRGINIA

BARBOURSVILLE VINEYARDS

The Zonin family of Barboursville in Albemarle County has been involved in viticulture since 1821. In 1976 they were the first to grow *vitis vinifera* industrially in the state of Virginia. The vineyards now consist of 38 acres producing about 13,000 gallons a year. Wines from Bar-

boursville include Chardonnay, Riesling, Gewürz-traminer, Merlot, Cabernet Sauvignon and Rosé Barboursville. All the wines are produced and bottled on the estate.

CHERMONT WINERY

John Sherman, a retired Navy carrier pilot, first became interested in wine when stationed in California and Europe. He began his vineyard in 1978 with plantings of Cabernet Sauvignon and Chardonnay and reached 10 acres in 1981. Another six acres will be added over the next few years. The first commercial harvest at Chermont was in 1981; the first Chardonnay was put on the market in 1982. When in full production, Chermont will produce about 2,000 cases a year of Riesling, Cabernet Sauvignon and Chardonnay.

Chermont Winery has 726 vines per acre (BELOW), *which are hand-harvested* (RIGHT). *The mansion at Ingleside Plantation* (ABOVE RIGHT) *dates from 1833.*

FARFELU VINEYARD

Farfelu was the first new vineyard for many years to receive a Virginia winery license. The vineyard is situated at the foothills of the Shenandoah Mountains in Rappahannock County. Although the first vines were planted by the Charles J. Raney family on Flint Hill in 1966, their first commercially available wines were released in 1976.

FARFELU
VIRGINIA
SEYVAL BLANC
VINEYARD

PRODUCED AND
BOTTLED BY
FARFELU VINEYARD
BW-VA-23
FLINT HILL,
RAPPAHANNOCK
COUNTY
VIRGINIA 22627
ALCOHOL 12%
BY VOLUME

The grapes from the Chambourcin, Chancellor, Chelois, de Chaunac, Millot, Seyval and Villard Blanc vines are used and blended to produce Farfelu Dry Red Wine which has a strong, full-bodied flavor, and also a dry, white Seyval Blanc, which is crisp and refreshing.

INGLESIDE PLANTATION

Vines were first planted at Ingleside on a trial basis in 1960, but it was not until 1980 that the present regional farm winery was established. The 20-acre vineyard is located in Westmoreland County, not far from the birthplace of George Washington. About 20,000 gallons of wine are produced each year from the 30 varieties of grapes grown on the plantation. Among the reds are Cabernet Sauvignon, Chancellor and Nouveau Red, a Beaujolais-type blend. A semi-sweet rosé and an apple wine are also made, as is a bottle-fermented Virginia sparkling wine.

LA ABRA FARM AND WINERY

Founded in 1973, La Abra is central Virginia's first estate winery since Prohibition. Located in the foothills of the Blue Ridge Mountains, the vineyards consist of 12 acres of French hybrids, used to produce wine under the Mountain Cove Vineyards label. This line includes Skyline White, Skyline Red and a Villard Blanc. Under the La Abra name, the winery also makes slightly more unusual varieties: apple and peach wine.

MEREDYTH VINEYARDS

Meredyth Vineyards lies in the historic foothills of the Bull Run Mountains, in the Piedmont region of northern Virginia. It is currently the largest commercial vineyard in the state, producing about 10,000 cases of wine each year. The

French hybrid and vinifera vines were planted in 1972; the first harvest was in 1975. Meredyth wines have been critically acclaimed and are widely distributed. Among the reds are Maréchal Foch, de Chaunac and Villard Noir; the whites include Seyval Blanc, Villard Blanc and Aurora Blanc. An interesting Rougeon Rosé is also made. All Meredyth wines are vintage-dated and most are estate-bottled.

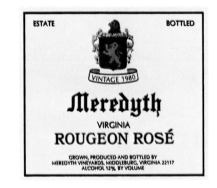

MONTDOMAINE CELLARS

Final planting on the 30-acre Montdomaine Cellars vineyard was completed in 1983. The new winery is the first estate winery in Albemarle County since Prohibition. It can produce 7,500 cases a year. Currently available wines from Montdomaine are an estate-bottled Chardonnay and an oak-aged Merlot. The Merlot is released under the Monticello Wine Company label.

RIGHT *Some winemakers choose to put their grapes into a hopper after they have been handpicked from the vineyards, rather than feeding them straight into a field crusher. This is to minimize oxidation and excessive contact between the skin and juice of the grape. The grapes are then poured from the hopper into a crusher-stemmer to separate them from their stems.*

NAKED MOUNTAIN VINEYARD

On the east slope of the Blue Ridge Mountains in Fauquier County, Naked Mountain Vineyard was planted in 1976. The winery began with the vintage of 1981, which produced 700 gallons. The goal is 10,000 gallons a year. The winery now offers Chardonnay, Sauvignon Blanc, Riesling and Claret made in the Medoc style. The 1981 Chardonnay and 1981 Sauvignon Blanc have both been well-received, winning bronze medals in the Eastern Wine Competition of 1982.

RAPIDAN RIVER VINEYARDS

In 1710, German settlers along the Rapidan River grew large amounts of European grapes. Disease overtook the vines, however, and the vineyards eventually failed. In 1978, Dr. Gerhard Guth, a surgeon from Hamburg, founded Rapidan River Vineyards in the rolling hills of Orange County. Since then there has been much activity at the vineyards and there are now 27,000 vinifera vines planted on 25 acres. The estate-grown and estate-bottled wines of Rapidan River Vineyards are

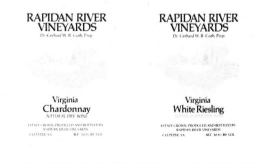

produced in the German tradition. The most popular wines include dry and semi-dry White Rieslings, as well as Chardonnay, Gewürztraminer and Pinot Noir. The vineyards are likely to expand further in the future.

ROSE BOWER VINEYARD AND WINERY

The first vines at Rose Bower, a small, country colonial house built in the eighteenth century, were planted in 1974. Today the vineyard covers six acres of both French hybrids and vinifera. The winery was licensed in 1979 and the first wines were sold in 1980. The vintage-dated wines of Rose Bower are offered directly from the estate in the manner of a small Burgundian chateau. Among those available is Nouveau Foch, made from Maréchal Foch grapes and in the manner of Beaujolais. Also made are Johannisberg Riesling, Chardonnay and Cabernet Sauvignon. Briery Lake is a white blend similar to the white Graves of Bordeaux; Hampden Forest is a blend of vinifera and hybrids resembling a dry claret.

SHENANDOAH VINEYARDS

Shenandoah Vineyards is nestled in a valley between the Blue Ridge and Shenandoah Mountains. The first winery in the area, Shenandoah now has 40 acres of vineyard producing Seyval Blanc, a delicate white table wine; Vidal, a spicier white wine; Chardonnay; Villard; Chancellor; Chambourcin, a full flavored claret type; de Chaunac and Johannisberg Riesling. They produce a medium dry Shenandoah Rosé and Shenandoah Blanc. Annual production is 25,000 gallons.

TRI-MOUNTAIN WINERY AND VINEYARDS

Tri-Mountain Winery is aptly named. This small, new winery is in the northern Shenandoah Valley in the cradle of three mountains — the Blue Ridge to the east, the Massanutten to the south and the Great North Mountain to the west. Annual production at the winery is about 7,000 gallons of seven different wines: Blue Ridge Rosé, Great North Mountain Concord, Massanutten White, Tri-Mountain Red, Cabernet Sauvignon, Seyval-Aligote and Apfelwein.

WOOLWINE WINERY

So new that its wines have been released only in very limited quantities, Woolwine Winery has 15 acres of French hybrids and five acres of vinifera planted at an elevation of 3,400 feet in the Rocky Knob area of southern Virginia. This region has been established as a viticultural area by the federal government. The first sales at Woolwine were in the summer of 1983; 1984 will see production rise to 5,000 gallons a year, with 30,000 gallons projected by 1987.

GLOSSARY

Acid The quality of tart freshness, the ability to age well; carried to extremes, undesirable and nearly undrinkable.

Aftertaste Back of the throat taste; lingering, it intimates complexity.

Alcohol A result of fermentation of sugar-containing liquids; chemically, C_2H_5OH.

Amontillado Dry sherry.

Amoroso Medium-dry sherry.

Aperitif Appetizer or before dinner drink.

Aroma The grape smell of a young wine.

Astringency A dryness in the mouth after quaffing highly tannic wines.

Balance The quality when all constituents in a wine are in harmony.

Binning Cellaring in bottles to allow development.

Blending Mixing two or more wines to obtain better and more uniform final result.

Body Tasters' term to indicate the consistency of *taste* in a wine partly due to alcoholic content.

Botrytis cinerea "Noble rot," a mold that attacks certain white wine grapes in the autumn before harvest; beneficial because it causes a water loss and a concentration of sugar producing elegant, sweet dessert wines.

Bouquet The smell which comes with maturity in wine, usually complex.

Breed The character of excellence in a fine wine.

Brut A very dry Champagne.

Capsule Metal or plastic protector for the bottle cork.

Cask Oak barrel for aging wines.

Cave Warehouse or cellar for storing wines.

Chaptalization The addition of sugar or grape must to the wine before fermentation; especially done in poor years when the grapes are deficient in natural sugar; outlawed in certain areas.

Clean Said of a wine that is refreshing.

Coarse Said of a wine that tastes crude and poorly vinified.

Complete Balanced and mature wine.

Complex "Scents-within-scents" quality of a wine suggestive of flowers, fruits, etc.; usually applied only to fine wines.

Corky Smell imparted to the wine by a moldy cork; very rare.

Crust Heavy sediment; usually applied to vintage port.

Decanting Transferring a wine from the bottle to another container; only necessary when the wine has thrown a sediment.

Deposit Normal sediment given off by a wine, particularly red, as it matures in the bottle.

Dry Opposite of sweet.

Earthy The taste of soil, characteristic of big red wines.

Eiswein Wine produced from perfectly ripened grapes that have been partially frozen on the vine. The result is a clean, intense white dessert wine. Once limited to Germany, it is being made increasingly in Washington and Oregon.

Elegance A wine of breed, finesse, style...classy.

Esters The volatile compounds produced by the combination of alcohol and organic acids. They give a wine its bouquet.

Estate-bottled Produced and bottled by the vineyard owner.

Extra Dry Term denoting a slightly sweet Champagne.

Fat Fleshy wine, almost too round and rich.

Fermentation The process in which sugars are turned into alcohol, carbon dioxide and other by-products.

Filter Clarification process; if done too vigorously, it will produce a flat, boring wine.

Fine To clarify by adding materials to the wine to precipitate sediment.

Finish The aftertaste of a wine.

Firm A wine of youth with style.

Flower As in *flor* (Spanish), a unique yeast that forms a top layer on dry sherries and gives them their special qualities.

Flowery An attractive perfume.

Fortified wines Those wines that are increased in alcoholic strength by the addition of a brandy. Sherry, port, etc., are examples.

Foxiness The pronounced grapey flavor of wines made from native eastern U.S. grapes (Delaware, Concord, Catawba, etc.)

Green Said of a very young wine, unfinished.

Gunflint Some white wines can only be described as "flinty," especially very dry whites.

Hard A very tannic young red wine.

Hydrometer Used to measure the density of alcoholic beverage.

Informing grape The principal grape giving a varietal its particular character; defined in the U.S. under law.

Isinglass A fining substance

made from fish gelatin.

Jeroboam A double magnum bottle holding 104 ounces or 4 bottles.

Lees The sediment in the bottom of a wine cask.
Lively Said of a wine that is fresh and shows signs of lasting.

Made and bottled by Legally means that up to 90 percent of the wine has been bought in bulk.
Magnum A double-sized bottle.
Metallic Just that; not necessarily a bad thing in itself in strong reds.
Méthode Champenoise A method of making champagne and sparkling wine. It is fermented twice, first in a cask as any wine; second, after bottling, the wine is racked until sediment comes against the cork. Then, the neck of the bottle is frozen; the sediment pops out when the cork is removed. A *dosage* or injection of grape sugar is added, and the wine is recorked. The addition of sugar causes a second fermentation to take place in bottle, and the resulting carbon dioxide is the bubbly we all cherish.
Mildew A disease attacking vines in especially wet weather.
Must Grape juice before and during fermentation.
Musty Bad smell, probably from an unsound wood barrel.

Oloroso Full-bodied, deep-colored sherries of a decidedly sweet nature.

Pasteurization A process similar to that applied to milk. Never used for fine wines as the process arrests any possible development and improvement by aging.

Produced and bottled by Legally means at least 75 percent of the wine so labeled was fermented at the winery.

Racking The drawing off of wine from one cask into another, leaving the lees or sediment behind.
Racy A wine that is exciting, fresh.
Refresh To add new wine to older wine in the cask.
Residual sugar The amount left after wine is not fermented completely dry. One percent is sweet.
Robe The glaze of color left in a glass from a particularly darkly pigmented red wine.
Rosé A light wine made by quick removal of the grape skins.

Sediment Natural deposits found mainly in red wines as they mature. Perfectly acceptable, the sediment can be the sign of something good to drink.
Supple Said of a wine that is not hard; however, it does not mean soft, and supple wines usually have a good bit of finish.
Sulfury The eggy smell of white wines where sulfur has been used as a preservative. If the bottle is left open for a half-hour, the smell will usually disappear.

Tannin Organic compounds found in red grape skins, stems and oak barrels. Astringent when young, such wines are given their longevity and ability to develop by tannins.
Tawny A paleness in port from repeated finings.

Varietal wine Named for the principal grape variety used. By law this must be at least 51 percent; as of 1983, 75 percent of the labeled variety must be used.

Vats Used for fermenting, they can be of wood, stainless steel, glass-lined concrete or concrete alone.
Vinosity The character of a wine, its balance of flavor, body, and bouquet.
Vintage The year in which the wine was bottled, marked on the label.
Viticulture The science (and art) of growing grapes.

Weeper A bottle that shows signs of leakage through the cork.
Woody The taste of a wine that has been aged too long in wood.

Yeast The plant organisms that cause fermentation.
Yeasty Usually found in young wines, yeastiness — detectable through smell — is a sign of partial bottle-fermentation and possible instability.

ADDRESSES

CALIFORNIA

Acacia Winery
2750 Las Amigas Road
Napa, California 94558

Ahlgren Vineyard
20320 Highway 9
Boulder Creek, California 95006

Alexander Valley Vineyards
8644 Highway 128
Healdsburg, California 95448

Almadén Vineyards
1530 Blossom Hill Road
San Jose, California 95118

Bargetto Winery
3535A North Main Street
Soquel, California 95073

Beaulieu Vineyard
1960 St. Helena Highway
Rutherford, California 94573

Boeger Winery
1709 Carson Road
Placerville, California 95667

David Bruce Winery
21439 Bear Creek Road
Los Gatos, California 95030

Buena Vista Winery and Vineyards
Old Winery Road
Sonoma, California 95476

Burgess Cellars
1180 Deer Park Road
St. Helena, California 94574

Davis Bynum Winery
8075 Westside Road
Healdsburg, California 95448

Cakebread Cellars
8300 St. Helena Highway
Rutherford, California 94573

Calera Wine Company
11300 Cienega Road
Hollister, California 95023

Callaway Vineyard & Winery
32720 Rancho California Road
Temecula, California 92390

Carneros Creek Winery
1285 Dealy Lane
Napa, California 94558

Cassayre-Forni Cellars
1271 Manley Lane
Rutherford,
California 94573

Chalone Vineyards
Box 855
Soledad, California 93960

Chateau Bouchaine
1075 Buchli Station Road
Napa, California 94558

Chateau Montelena
1429 Tubbs Lane
Calistoga, California 94515

Chateau St. Jean Vineyards and Winery
8555 Sonoma Highway
Kenwood, California 95452

The Christian Brothers
Mont La Salle
Napa, California 94558

Clos du Bois
5 Fitch Street
Healdsburg,
California 95448

Clos du Val
5330 Silverado Trail
Napa, California 94558

Colony Wines
Asti, California 95413

Concannon Vineyards
4590 Tesla Road
Livermore, California 94550

Congress Springs Vineyards
23600 Congress Springs Road
Saratoga, California 95070

Cresta Blanca Winery
2399 North State Street
Ukiah, California 95482

Cuvaison Winery
4550 Silverado Trail
Calistoga, California 94515

De Loach Vineyards
1791 Olivet Road
Santa Rosa, California 95401

Diablo Vista Winery
674 East H Street
Benicia, California 94510

Diamond Creek Vineyards
1500 Diamond Mountain Road
Calistoga, California 94515

Domaine Chandon
California Drive
Yountville, California 94599

Dry Creek Vineyards
3770 Lambert Bridge Road
Healdsburg, California 95448

Durney Vineyard
Box 222016
Carmel Valley, California 93924

Edna Valley Vineyard
Biddle Ranch Road
San Luis Obispo,
California 93401

Far Niente Winery
Box 327
Oakville, California 94562

Fetzer Vineyards
1150 Bel Arbres Road
Redwood Valley,
California 95470

Firestone Vineyards
Box 244
Los Olivos, California 93441

Fisher Vineyards
6200 St. Helena Road
Santa Rosa, California 95404

Foppiano Vineyards
12781 Old Redwood Highway
Healdsburg,
California 95448

Fortina Winery
4525 Hecker Pass Highway
Gilroy, California 95020

Franciscan Vineyards
Box 407
Rutherford,
California 94573

Freemark Abbey Winery
3022 St. Helena Highway
St. Helena, California 94574

E & J Gallo Winery
Modesto,
California 95353

Glen Ellen Winery
1883 London Ranch Road
Glen Ellen, California 95442

Grand Cru Vineyards
One Vintage Lane
Glen Ellen, California 95442

Grgich Hills Cellars
1829 St. Helena Highway
Rutherford, California 94573

Guenoc Winery
21000 Butts Canyon Road
Middletown, California 95461

**Gundlach-Bundschu
Wine Company**
3775 Thornsberry Road
Vineburg, California 95487

Hacienda Wine Cellars
1000 Vineyard Lane
Sonoma, California 95476

Hanzell Vineyards
18596 Lomita Avenue
Sonoma, California 95476

Heitz Wine Cellars
436 St. Helena Highway South
St. Helena, California 94574

Hoffman Mountain Ranch
Adelaide Road, Star Route
Paso Robles, California 93446

**Hop Kiln Winery
at Griffin Vineyard**
6050 Westside Road
Healdsburg, California 95448

Husch Vineyards
4900 Star Route
Philo, California 95466

Inglenook Vineyards
Box 19
Rutherford, California 94573

Iron Horse Vineyards
9786 Ross Station Road
Sebastopol, California 95472

Jekel Vineyard
40155 Walnut Avenue
Greenfield, California 93927

**Johnson' Alexander
Valley Winery**
8333 State Highway 128
Healdsburg, California 95448

Kalin Cellars
1729 A Toyon Road
Lafayette, California 94549

Robert Keenan Winery
3660 Spring Mountain Road
St. Helena, California 94574

The Konocti Winery
Highway 29 at Thomas Drive
Kelseyville, California 95451

**Hanns Kornell
Champagne Cellars**
Box 249
St. Helena, California 94574

Charles Krug Winery
Box 191
St. Helena, California 94574

Long Vineyards
Box 50
St. Helena, California 94574

Lytton Springs Winery
650 Lytton Springs Road
Healdsburg, California 95448

Markham Winery
2812 North St. Helena Highway
St. Helena, California 94574

Mark West Vineyards
7000 Trenton-Healdsburg Road
Forestville, California 95436

Louis M. Martini Winery
Box 112
St. Helena, California 94574

Paul Masson Vineyards
13150 Saratoga Avenue
Saratoga, California 95070

Mastantuono Winery
Route 1, Willow Creek Road
Paso Robles, California 93446

Matanzas Creek Winery
6097 Bennett Valley Road
Santa Rosa, California 95404

Mayacamas Vineyards
1155 Lokoya Road
Napa, California 94558

**McDowell Valley
Vineyards**
3811 Highway 175
Hopland, California 95449

**Milano Vineyards
and Winery**
14594 South Highway 101
Hopland, California 95449

**Mill Creek Vineyards
and Winery**
1401 Westside Road
Healdsburg, California 95448

Mirassou Vineyards
3000 Aborn Road
San Jose, California 95135

Robert Mondavi Winery
7801 St. Helena Highway
Oakville, California 94562

R. Montali Winery
719 Allston Way
Berkeley, California

Monterey Peninsula Winery
2999 Monterey
Salinas Highway
Monterey, California 93940

The Monterey Vineyard
800 South Alta Street
Gonzales, California 93926

Monteviña Wines
Route 2
Plymouth, California 95669

J.W. Morris Wineries
4060 Pike Lane
Concord, California 94520

Mount Eden Vineyards
22020 Mount Eden Road
Saratoga, California 95070

Mount Veeder Winery
1999 Mount Veeder Road
Napa, California 94558

Navarro Vineyards
5601 Highway 128
Philo, California 95466

Novitiate Winery
300 College Avenue
Los Gatos, California 95030

Parducci Wine Cellars
501 Parducci Road
Ukiah, California 95482

J. Pedroncelli Winery
1220 Canyon Road
Geyserville,
California 95441

Joseph Phelps Vineyards
200 Taplin Road
St. Helena, California 94574

Piper Sonoma
Box 368
Windsor, California 95492

Preston Vineyards
9282 West Dry Creek Road
Healdsburg,
California 95448

Quail Ridge Winery
1055 Atlas Peak Road
Napa, California 94558

Martin Ray Vineyards
22000 Mt. Eden Road
Saratoga, California 95070

Raymond Vineyard and Cellar
849 Zinfandel Lane
St. Helena, California 94574

Ridge Vineyards
17100 Monte Bello Road
Cupertino, California 95015

Roudon-Smith Vineyards
2364 Bean Creek Road
Santa Cruz, California 95066

Round Hill Vineyards
1097 Lodi Lane
St. Helena, California 94574

Rutherford Hill Winery
3022 St. Helena Highway
St. Helena, California 94574

Rutherford Vintners
Box 238
Rutherford, California 94573

St. Clement Vineyards
2867 St. Helena Highway North
St. Helena, California 94574

Sanford & Benedict Vineyards
Santa Rosa Road
Lompoc, California 93436

San Martin Winery
12900 Monterey Road
San Martin, California 95046

Santa Cruz Mountain Vineyard
2300 Jarvis Road
Santa Cruz, California 95065

Santino Winery
Route 2
21A Steiner Road
Plymouth, California 95669

Schramsberg Vineyards
Calistoga, California 94515

Sebastiani Vineyards
389 Fourth Street East
Sonoma, California 95476

Shafer Vineyards
6154 Silverado Trail
Napa, California 94558

Shown & Sons Vineyards
8643 Silverado Trail
Rutherford, California 94573

Sierra Vista Winery
4560 Cabernet Way
Placerville, California 95667

Simi Winery
16275 Healdsburg Avenue
Healdsburg, California 95448

Smith-Madrone Vineyards and Winery
4022 Spring Mountain Road
St. Helena, California 94574

Sonoma Vineyards
Old Redwood Highway
Windsor, California 95492

Sotoyome Winery
641 Limerick Lane
Healdsburg,
California 95448

Souverain
Box 528 Geyserville,
California 95441

Spring Mountain Vineyards
2805 Spring Mountain Road
St. Helena, California 94574

Stag's Leap Wine Cellars
Napa, California 94558

P. and M. Staiger Winery
1300 Hopkins Gulch Road
Boulder Creek, California 95006

Robert Stemmler Winery
3805 Lambert Bridge Road
Healdsburg, California 95448

Sterling Vineyards
1111 Dunaweal Lane
Calistoga, California 94515

Stevenot Winery
San Domingo Ranch
Murphys, California 95247

Stonegate Winery
1183 Dunaweal Lane
Calistoga, California 94515

Sutter Home Winery
277 St. Helena Highway South
St. Helena, California 94574

Sycamore Creek Vineyards
12775 Uvas Road
Morgan Hill, California 95037

Taylor California Cellars
Gonzales, California 93926

Trefethen Vineyards
1160 Oak Knoll Avenue
Napa, California 94558

**Trentadue Vineyards
and Winery**
19170 Redwood Highway
Geyserville, California 95441

Turgeon & Lohr Winery
1000 Lenzen Avenue
San Jose, California 95126

Ventana Vineyard
Box G
Soledad, California 93960

Villa Mt. Eden
Oakville Crossroads
Oakville, California 94562

Wente Bros.
5565 Tesla Road
Livermore, California 94550

Woodbury Winery
San Rafael, California 94901

Zaca Mesa Winery
Box 547
Los Olivos, California 93441

ZD Wines
8383 Silverado Trail
Napa, California 94558

NEW YORK

Benmarl Vineyards
Marlboro-on-the-Hudson,
New York 12542

Brimstone Hill Vineyards
R.D. 2, Box 142
Pine Bush, New York 12566

Bully Hill Vineyards
Hammondsport,
New York 14840

Cagnasso Winery
Marlboro, New York 12542

Casa Larga Vineyards
2287 Turk Hill Road
Fairport, New York 14450

**Cascade Mountain
Vineyards**
Flint Hill Road
Amenia, New York 12501

**Chateau Esperanza
Winery**
Route 54A, Box 76
Bluff Point, New York 14417

Cottage Vineyards
Marlboro-on-the-Hudson,
New York 12542

DeMay Wine Cellars
Hammondsport,
New York 14840

**Four Chimneys
Farm Winery**
Hall Road
Himrod-on-Seneca,
New York 14842

Glenora Wine Cellars
Dundee, New York 14837

Great Western Winery
Hammondsport,
New York 14840

Hargrave Vineyard
Alvah's Lane
Cutchogue, New York 11935

Heron Hill Vineyards
Hammonsport, New York 14840

Johnson Estate Wines
Box 52
Westfield, New York 14787

Lenz Vineyards
Main Road
Peconic, New York 11958

McGregor Vineyard Winery
5503 Dutch Street
Dundee, New York 14837

Needleman Winery
New Suffolk, New York 11956

Northeast Vineyard
Silver Mountain Road
Millertone, New York 12546

North Salem Vineyards
Route 2
North Salem, New York 10560

Plane's Cayuga Vineyard
Route 89, R.D. 2
Ovid, New York 14521

Rotolo & Romeo Wines
234 Rochester Street
Avon, New York 14414

Taylor Wine Company
Hammondsport,
New York 14840

Valley Vineyards
Oregon Trail Road
Walker Valley, New York 12588

Wickham Vineyards Ltd.
1 Wine Place
Hector, New York 14841

Hermann J. Wiemer
Vineyard Route 14, Box 4
Dundee, New York 14837

Windsor Vineyards
104 Western Avenue
Marlboro, New York 12542

WASHINGTON

Chateau Ste. Michelle
One Stimson Lane
Woodinville, Washington 98072

Hinzerling Vineyards
1520 Sheridan Avenue
Prosser, Washington 99350

Lost Mountain Winery
730 Lost Mountain Road
Sequim, Washington 98382

Preston Wine Cellars
Star Route, Box 1234
Tri-Cities, Washington 99302

Tucker Cellars
Route 1, Box 1696
Sunnyside, Washington 98944

Manfred Vierthaller Winery
17136 Highway 410 East
Sumner, Washington 98390

Worden's Washington
Winery
7217 West 45th
Spokane, Washington 99204

Yakima River Winery
North River Road
Prosser, Washington 99350

OREGON

Alpine Vineyards
Green Peak Road
Alpine, Oregon 97456

Amity Vineyards
Route 1, Box 348B
Amity, Oregon 97101

Chateau Benoit
Route 1, Box 29B-1
Carlton, Oregon 97111

Côte des Colombes
Vineyard Box 266
Banks, Oregon 97106

Elk Cove Vineyards
Route 3, Box 23
Gaston, Oregon 97119

The Eyrie Vineyards
Box 204
Dundee, Oregon 97115

Forgeron Vineyard
89697 Sheffler Road
Elmira, Oregon 97437

Henry Winery
Box 26
Umpqua, Oregon 97486

Hinman Vineyards
27012 Briggs Hill Road
Eugene, Oregon 97405

Knudsen Erath Winery
Worden Hill Road
Dundee, Oregon 97115

Nehalem Bay
Wine Company
34967 Highway 53
Nehalem, Oregon 97131

Oak Knoll Winery
Route 6, Box 184
Hillsboro, Oregon 97123

Ponzi Vineyards
Route 1, Box 842
Beaverton, Oregon 97007

Serendipity Cellars Winery
15275 Dunn Forest Road
Monmouth, Oregon 97361

Shafer Vineyard Cellars
Star Route, Box 269
Forest Grove, Oregon 97116

Siskiyou Vineyards
6220 Caves Highway
Cave Junction, Oregon 97523

Sokol Blosser Winery
Blanchard Lane
Dundee, Oregon 97115

Tualatin Vineyards
Route 1, Box 339
Forest Grove, Oregon 97116

IDAHO

Facelli Vineyards
Route 2, Peckham Road
Wilder, Idaho 83676

Ste. Chapelle Vineyards
Route 4, Box 775
Caldwell, Idaho 83605

ARKANSAS

Wiederkehr Wine Cellars
Wiederkehr Village
Altus, Arkansas 72821

CONNECTICUT

Hamlet Hill Vineyards
Pomfret, Connecticut 06258

Hopkins Vineyard
Hopkins Road in Warren
New Preston,
Connecticut 06777

Stonecrop Vineyards
Box 151A, RR 2
Stonington, Connecticut 06378

INDIANA

Oliver Wine Company
8024 North Highway 37
Bloomington, Indiana 47401

MARYLAND

Boordy Vineyards
12820 Long Green Pike
Hydes, Maryland 21082

Montbray Wine Cellars
818 Silver Run Valley Road
Westminster, Maryland 21157

Ziem Vineyards
Route 1
Fairplay, Maryland 21733

MASSACHUSSETTS

Commonwealth Winery
Cordage Park
Plymouth, Massachusetts 02360

MICHIGAN

Boskydel Vineyard
Route 1, Box 522
Lake Leelanau, Michigan 49653

**L. Mawby
Vineyards/Winery**
Box 237
Suttons Bay, Michigan 49682

**Tabor Hill Vineyard
and Winecellar**
Route 2, Box 720
Buchanan, Michigan 49107

MISSOURI

Bias Vineyards and Winery
Berger, Missouri 63014

Mount Pleasant Vineyards
Augusta, Missouri 63332

Reis Winery
Route 4, Box 133
Licking, Missouri 65542

The Winery of the Abbey
Cuba, Missouri 65453

NEW JERSEY

Tewksbury Wine Cellars
Burrell Road
Lebanon, New Jersey 08833

OHIO

Hafle Vineyards
2369 Upper Valley Pike
Springfield, Ohio 45502

PENNSYLVANIA

Allegro Vineyards
R.D. 2, Box 64
Brogue, Pennsylvania 17307

Stephen Bahn Winery
Goram Road
Brogue, Pennsylvania 17309

**Kolln Vineyards
and Winery**
R.D. 1, Box 439
Bellefonte,
Pennsylvania 16823

Lapic Winery
682 Tulip Drive
New Brighton,
Pennsylvania 15066

**Lembo Vineyards
and Winery**
34 Valley Street
Lewistown,
Pennsylvania 17044

**Mount Hope.
Estate and Winery**
Box 685
Cornwall, Pennsylvania 17016

**York Springs
Vineyard and Winery**
R.D. 1, Box 194
York Springs,
Pennsylvania 17372

VIRGINIA

Barboursville Vineyards
Box F
Barboursville, Virginia 22923

Chermont Winery
Route 1, Box 59
Esmont, Virginia 22937

Farfelu Vineyard
Flint Hill, Virginia 22627

Ingleside Plantation
Box 1038
Oak Grove, Virginia 22443

La Abra Farm and Winery
State Route 651
Lovington, Virginia 22949

Meredyth Vineyards
Box 347
Middleburg, Virginia 22117

Montdomaine Cellars
Route 6, Box 168A
Charlottesville, Virginia 22901

**Naked Mountain
Vineyard**
Box 131
Markham, Virginia 22643

Rapidan River Vineyards
Route 4, Box 199
Culpeper, Virginia 22701

**Rose Bower
Vineyard and Winery**
Hampden-Sydney,
Virginia 23943

Shenandoah Vineyards
Edinburg, Virginia 22824

**Tri-Mountain
Winery and Vineyards**
Route 1, Box 254
Middletown, Virginia 22645

Woolwine Winery
Box 100
Woolwine, Virginia 24185

INDEX

Page numbers in *italic* refer to captions and illustrations.